The Big Book of Scroll Saw for Beginners

A Woodworker Guide to Crafting 20 Woodworking Scroll Saw Patterns, Designs and Projects Plus Scrolling Tools and Tips to Get You Started

By

Luke Byrd

Disclaimer

This publication is designed to provide competent and reliable information regarding the subject matter covered. However, the views expressed in this publication are those of the author alone, and should not be taken as expert instruction or professional advice. The reader is responsible for his or her own actions.

The author hereby disclaims any responsibility or liability whatsoever that is incurred from the use or application of the contents of this publication by the purchaser or reader. The purchaser or reader is hereby responsible for his or her own actions.

Table of Contents

Introduction

Scroll saws may look very complicated with all of their big components and endless buttons, but then, they create one of the best woodwork projects to have ever existed. Good enough, the device is very simple to operate on as; all the once complex features can just be activated with simple button flicks. With a scroll saw device, you can make gifts for your friends and families, spice up that severely decorated room in your house and even earn money from your crafts.

Scroll saws are devices fixed on a table or regular surfaces with motors attached to them. The motors usually help keep the blade running and that motion is what cuts through your wooden plaque—it could be pinewood, Baltic Birch, or Maple. The tools are cheap and the art is interesting enough for you to live big from it.

However, before you get to do that, you have to go through the rigorous learning process involved in the art of scroll saw. This book will guide you through the steps you will need to take for each project, several techniques, tips, well-detailed explanations, and a thousand more things you don't want to ever miss. You will also be guided on the kind of wood to get and how well to decorate and finish the wood into something really beautiful, whether you have handled a scroll saw device before or not. Most importantly, you would eventually find it very easy to convert the theories you learn here into beautiful and realistic projects!

At the end, you will come out as a professional and seasoned scroll artist.

So then, fasten your reading belts and enjoy the drive to being a professional scroll artist.

Chapter 1

Essentials of Scroll Saw

What is a Scroll Saw?

Just as the name implies, a scroll saw is a saw that cuts designs into materials by scrolling into them. It works as a sewing machine would, and if you already know how to use that machine, the scroll saw would be a total work-over for you. It can cut through several kinds of materials like wood, leather, nylon, anything, as long as it's not too dense. It doesn't work with dense materials because it has a very fine blade that could easily get dented when too much pressure is applied.

Now, let's go into more intricate details of what a scroll saw is. It is a device that is powered either by electricity or mechanical pedaling to cut out sophisticated designs and outlines on wood or any other material. Scroll saws can also be briefly described as narrow sawing blades that are housed within wooden compartments. If you have never seen a scroll saw before, you can imagine it as a sewing machine because they share many similarities. The blade runs vertically like the needle in a sewing machine, and you can use your feet to run the pedals while your hands work on adjusting and moving the material you want to cut designs through.

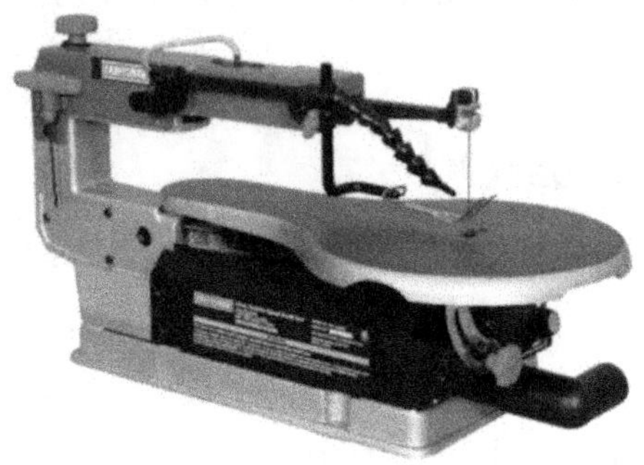

The blade of a scroll saw is known as a reciprocating blade. These kinds of blades work on a push and pull principle when cutting designs on wood. So, when the saw begins to work, the blade pushes through the material first and then pulls it out. You have to guide it to the next spot and have it repeat that same procedure. Wood crafters most cherish this feature as it helps them achieve higher rates of meticulousness when working. They can take a short break between the cuts and observe how well the cuts are being made. So, in much simpler terms, you can also describe the blade of a scroll saw as one that works in an up and down motion.

So, generally, a scroll saw is a simple device that makes clean cuts into materials. They have specified roles they play, and if you learned their mechanisms, you could come up with thousands of amazing craftwork.

History of the Scroll Saw

The scroll saw is a device that has undergone thousands of reformations over the years, all by different people who ended up using the saw for one thing or the other. Back in the days when there was almost nothing called technology, the wood crafters cut into the wood by holding the blades in their hands. They used the saw's blade just like you'd use a razor. The blades then were in the shapes of knives, and so, they couldn't be used for intricate designs. The crafters then felt that if the saw was going to look like a knife, the blade had to be relatively dense enough to be bent by the pressure applied to it by their fingers.

At that time, the use of scroll saws was referred to as Fretwork. Fretwork is an art that involves a crafter carving out ornamental designs on wood or any other regular surface with the use of fretsaws, coping saws, or scroll saws. So, since the scroll saw used then looked like the rest of the saws listed above, the crafters decided to tag it under Fretwork's crafts.

So, the early crafts on the Egyptians' furniture and the Romans' were all one with the scroll saw, which was more or less a knife.

However, a consequential reformation started when a craft man from Germany came up with the idea of using much more narrow and finer blades. He reasoned that if they were ever going to succeed at making more delicate cuts in their craft materials, they needed a blade that wasn't heavy or hard to manipulate. His theory then was in the similitude of the thinness of the metallic hands of a clock.

The German's theory was accepted, but then, there came how they were supposed to handle the blade. If the thin blades were fixed to the handle of knives, they'd snap into two! So, a Parisian crafter, Mr. Boule, introduced to them the idea of fixing the blade to the frame of a fret saw shaped into a 'U.' He called this invention the Buhl saw. So, with this, they could apply force on the wooden handle and still not cause any damage to the blade. The crafters then saw this new idea as ingenious, and it spread around like wildfire. Everyone began to use the Buhl saw. However, this scroll saw make-shift was still classified as a Fretwork.

In the middle of the 1800s, the Fretwork craft got introduced into the United States as Sorrento, another term that meant wood carving. 'Sorrento' was used because the art of wood carving had dominated a particular area in Italy. Almost every home then had the Buhl saw.

In 1860, the Buhl saw had already undergone a thousand other modifications and existed in the United States as mechanically powered saws. The crafters could operate the device by using their foot to paddle the device, their hand to spin the knobs, or their legs to pedal it quickly into motion. This stage was the time it began to look like a sewing machine. In this time phase, the world began to open up to the use of fretsaws to cut designs on wood. It became a hobby and a means of livelihood for so many people.

The people who lived in the Victorian era used scroll saws to design gingerbread outlines on wood to decorate their porches. The tool was also used to produce clock designs, ornate picture frames, and designs on ornaments.

In 1920, scroll saws became so popular that manufacturers like Barnes, Star, Hobbies, and even New Rogers began to produce them. Today, scroll saws have taken over forty different forms, each with its specified function. A clear difference has also been introduced between coping saws, jigsaws, band saws, fret saws, and scroll saws. Scroll saws make neater cuts than jigsaws and are easier to use than coping saws or fret saws. Band saws function for the dense materials used in carpentry, while scroll saws can only work on less dense materials. The band saw also works continuously while a scroll saw stops at intervals since its blade is reciprocated.

Most Common Types of Scroll Saws

Just like it was pointed earlier, there are over fifty different scroll saws, and now, it is time for us to discuss the commonly used ones.

Parallel Arm

The parallel arm saw is a saw that was first designed as far back as 1870, and you'd see that it has fewer components that work to keep the blade moving up and down. This saw is one of the few scroll saws that pose a little risk to the people that use it.

In a parallel arm scroll saw, you will find two arms parallel to each other with fulcrums holding them in place at their middles. They are connected at the back of the machine by a backlink and in front. The arms have grips for the saw blade that holds them together, thereby completing the outline of a parallelogram.

The lower arm is fixed to the motor that lies beneath the table of the parallel arm scroll saw. The parallel arm scroll saw is driven by an electric motor whose speed can be varied to meet different craftworks' requirements. The electric motor is connected to the lower arm with a crank rolled by the motor itself.

The cutting saw is usually fixed to the side between the blade that comes out longer. This method goes a long way to reduce the oscillatory motion of the arms. That's why the parallel arm system's components must be made with cast iron so that the instability of the parts can be countered.

This scroll saw is best for making vertical cuts on wood or any other material since the blade truly moves in an up and down style. It's also one of the safest because the upper arm will break off the parallelogram structure once the blade breaks, thereby causing the machine to stop at once.

C-Arm

The C-arm scroll saw is a saw that has a C-shape. It also looks much like a vise with a screw mouth at the top. The ends of the C-arms scroll saw were designed so that they hold the blade in place. The arms are fixed together with one fulcrum, which has contributed immensely to the saw's straight and clean cuts.

C-arms are very violent in their cuttings and very fast to cut with, but then, you'd need to be adequately skilled with it before you can get the kind of accurate outlines that you desire. When used on thick materials, you would notice the roughness of the outlines and the edges cut. However, if used on thinner materials, you wouldn't notice the saw's inaccurate cuts.

The C-arm saw is mostly used by artists that do designs that interlink closely together like you would have in fretwork designs. With the tool, they can do several things other woodwork tools cannot handle, like cutting deeper and smaller curves and bends.

However, this blade isn't as safe as the parallel arm saw because the moment the blade breaks, the upper part of the blade continues to move up and down unless you power off the motor running it. And this can be fatal if you are careless with the placement of your fingers.

Double Parallel Link Arm

This type of scroll saw is a device that is the current model being used in the world of craft today. It looks like the parallel arm saw, but more components work to drive the saw. It also vibrates less than the parallel arm saw. This saw has two arms that lie parallel to each other. The arms are connected at the back of the machine with a backlink and at the front is a blade held between the mouths.

The arms move in smooth oscillations, thereby causing the blade to move in the process. The backlink is connected to the device's motor with a crank to a variable speed electric motor. The body of the arms and the motor of any double parallel link arm must be made of cast iron as this counteracts the issue of easily displaced blades.

Rigid Arm

This saw is different from the ones mentioned above because it is not mobile. Saws like this one that works under a particular leave of strain have stiff and taut blades that cut with very high precision levels. This saw was commonly used between the 1920s and the 1980s before the parallel saws eventually came up.

The rigid arm scroll saw has a spring system fixed to the upper arm of the device. The blade is then attached to this particular upper arm. This device overall works to provide a vertical stroke that is deep and true. It would have been one saw to have received a lot of approval world-wide if not for a few issues it had. For example, powering the device to get a true up and down motion of the blade was very difficult. The blade was only under the full effects of tension when it neared the bottom, which wasn't effective for making deep cuts.

Uses of the Scroll Saw

1. The scroll saw is used to make detailed cuts, outlines, and patterns on materials like wood and leather.
2. It can also be used for carving wood and ivory to create art pieces like wooden statues and scrolls.
3. Scroll saws can be used for wooden tags and jigsaw puzzle blocks.
4. Scroll saws can be used to inscribe dovetail joints in wooden plaques.
5. Intarsia: This is a piece of art that involves laying fields of different colors and textures together on a platform where they match in the rhythm and

contrast nicely. The art makes use of wood plaques of various shapes and sizes to form mosaic-like graphics. These wood plaques are usually cut into the desired patterns with the use of the scroll saw.

6. Marquetry: This is another craftwork engineered towards forming decorative designs, images, and patterns with an already cut veneer. Veneers are pieces of wood that are attached to wooden surfaces to make them look less severe. These veneers are usually cut with the scroll saw.

7. Signs and templates: Templates are craft tools that can transfer letterings, fonts, and symbols to several surfaces. The templates are mostly materials made of wood or leather. Now, upon these materials are carved shapes and curves that aid in the transfer of the lettering. Scroll saw usually work to make these intricate curves.

8. The scroll saw can be used to cut through angles of ninety and more.

9. The scroll saw can help you cut out zig-zag patterns and circles into the wood.

10. Scroll saws can make mitered edges.

11. Scroll saws can be used for fretwork designs.

Using the Scroll Saw

Scroll saws may have a thousand screws, buttons, knobs, and components, but then, the last thing you should think of is whether it is challenging to operate or not, i.e., they are very easy to manipulate and are beginner-friendly. If you ever tried using a sewing machine, working with this wouldn't be difficult since the two devices work almost similar to each other.

Let's go through the various steps that would guide you on how to use a scroll saw.

- Cut the wooden plaque you will be working with to the size of your scroll saw's table. Here, you will have to know how long the throat of your saw is. The throat is the distance between the saw blade's tip and the end of the frame of the saw. If your scroll saw has a throat of 17 inches and a wooden plaque that measures 20 inches, you might have to reduce the size to something below 17 inches. This will ensure that you can easily control the wooden plaque in any direction you want.

- Now, the next step is determining how you want to outline your design. You could choose to draw it on the wood with a pencil or staple to the wood a sheet of paper containing the design's outline with glue. You could also use an aerosol adhesive to fix the outline to the wood.

P.S: Beginners should stick to using simple designs at first. For example, you could work with the outline of a leaf or star-shaped design. You should also make sure that your pencil outlines are sharp so that you can easily see them while cutting through the wood, if you are using pencils, that is.

- Wear your safety equipment before you get your hands on that scroll saw! Goggles will protect your eyes from wood dust and broken blades that could suddenly jump out of place while a motor powers the device. Overalls will protect your skin from irritation by the minuscule sawdust particles.

- Make sure the scroll saw sits right on your work table. To learn how to bolt, screw, and clamp the device down on your work table, follow the manufacturers' instructions.

- You should also make sure that the blade of the saw is firmly fixed to the table.

- To check for the tension in the blade, you can pluck it like you'd do the strings of a guitar. If it has the right tension, it will make a sharp ping sound. You can also check for the tension in the blade by pressing your finger to the middle of the blade. A blade under the right degree of tension will not move more than ⅛ inches in any direction.

  To find the right tension, work on a pressure that isn't so much that the blade snaps into two or bends slightly at the middle. You can also continue to adjust it while making sure to follow the manufacturer's instructions.

- Turn on the scroll saw after ensuring that the blade is tightly secured. Ensure that the moving blade isn't in contact with the wooden plaque when you first turn it on.

- You can try out the effectiveness of the blade on a scrap piece of wood first. If you are working with a thin material, make sure you set the device to run at a slow speed. You can even set the scroll saw to a very slow speed regardless of the density of the material you are working with. Then, you can adjust it as time goes on.

  P.S: As a beginner, you should always work with a scroll saw that operates at a slow speed. It will help you to control the actions of the saw easily.

- You can now begin to carefully push the design towards the moving blade with both of your hands. Ensure the area of the wooden plaque that you push towards the blade first is the point that begins your design's outline.

- Hold the wood firmly to the table of the scroll saw and then move it carefully towards the moving blade. If you need to adjust anything, use your forefingers and one of your thumbs. The other thumb shouldn't be on the wood as you guide it.

- When you have to turn around an angle of ninety in cutting your design, pull the wooden plaque away from the moving blade in a direction towards you. Then, rotate the wood so that the blade faces the new line you want to cut through, adjacent to the one you previously cut.

  P.S: The step above is entirely unnecessary if you work with a spiral blade that cuts through any angle or direction.

- If you cannot adequately follow your design outlines, reduce the speed of your saw's blade.

- Finish your work by first turning off the scroll saw. You should also remove the paper you glued to it shortly after and then smoothen the edges with sandpaper.

- Coat your work with shots of lacquer spray.

Chapter 2

Scroll Saw Tips and Tricks

If anyone is going to make the best use of their scroll saw, they'd need to know a few tips and tricks that have been noted by others who have handled the device.

Let's go through a few of them now.

- Ensure to scan the blade of your scroll saw device for any damage before using it. Also, make sure that it is under the right tension. These activities are things you must do before starting with your cutting as they are very vital!

  If you want your scroll saw to work at a degree of maximum efficiency, the blades have to be checked. Each project you might do may require its blade, so you have to see that you are using what is right for your project. If you know you will be making a lot of curves and cutting through many angles, you shouldn't use normal blades. Spiral blades function best for this purpose.

You should also make sure you check the size of the blade you are working with! Each project usually would require a blade of a particular size. You shouldn't use just one blade for all of your projects. For a wood plaque that is about ⅛ inches thick, stick with a grade two or grade three blade. The smaller the grade of a blade, the smaller the blade is. To a wooden plaque about ¾ inches thick, use either a grade 5 or grade 7 blade. The higher the grade of a blade, the thicker the wood it can cut through.

Small blades will slowly cut through wood, so you shouldn't try to overwork them by increasing their speed. If you do so, you could end up with rough cuttings. You should also use small blades to cut the delicate parts of your designs!

As regards the tension on your saw's blade, you have to bear in mind that a blade that's held loosely by the saw's clamp would not cut through anything. It would just keep slipping out of the clamp as you work. If the blade is also held too tensely, it could end up getting broken or bent.

So, to correct the tension on your blade to the right levels, you could use the knob on your sawing device to adjust the tension until you get what is right for your project if your scroll saw doesn't give this knob. However, you could pluck the blade at its middle and listen to the plucking sound it makes—something very similar to the sound the guitar strings make when they are being plucked. If the sound comes out with a very high frequency, it means the blade is too tense. If the sound comes out with a very low frequency, it means the blade is too loose.

To find the perfect frequency, you could use a guitar's tubing device or software that can listen to the sound made by the blade and tell you how tuned it is. But then, as you continue working with your scroll saw, you'd eventually get used to the sounds the blades make when they're plucked.

- If you decide to use wood as the cutting material, make sure it's dry enough first. If anything in the form of fluid pours on it, quickly wipe it with a dry cloth and then leave the wooden plaque to dry.

Even if the fluid didn't spill across the wooden plaque surface you plan on using for your project, ensure that you dry it before actually using it. Why? Before you bought the wood plaque, it could have had contact with some fluid lying around. You wouldn't know that.

Drying your wood will help your blades run smoothly through the wood without missing any important parts or areas.

- When working with the saw blade, ensure that the table is leveled with your midriff whether you are standing or sitting. That way, it would be easier for you to see what you are doing and, in turn, manage it well. Some scroll saws come with an adjustable table, which can be tilted either towards the right or the left until you reach an inclination of 45°.

As you tilt the table to the area of your midriff, ensure that the blade is in a position that falls in line with the table. It shouldn't be leaning towards the right or left. This will only contribute to you getting a sloppy or an uneven cut. If you see that your blade is bent, you might have to readjust the tension again. It might be under too much pressure. You could also check to see if the blade has been damaged.

- When working, make sure that you get good lighting to give you a clearer vision when cutting. It will help you cut through the design outlines and then have cut with high quality. Most scroll saws already have lighting systems built within them, so you needn't bother about lighting issues.

  However, if your scroll saw doesn't have one fitted with it or probably has one whose brightness isn't enough for you to see with, you could choose to get a LED or bulb.

- Ensure that you run an abrasive across your wooden plaque before cutting through it.

- To prevent your wooden plaque from splitting up in the insides or around the edges, start your cutting by drilling a hole into the wood. Split edges can result in your entire project getting ruined.

  There's a helpful tip you could work with when handling thin pieces of wood, though. Place a wood scrap below the thin wood you want to work with. The scrap wood will serve as a buttress for the actual one and then take in all the pressure exerted by the blade on the wood's squares. The buttress wood is usually there for balancing and supporting the actual wood.

- When cutting through thick pieces of wood, run through the blades of the device slowly. If the blade is working too fast, the friction between its tip and the wood could result in you stirring up so much heat that it ends up getting burnt. Your blades, even though string, could end up getting bent or broken. The secret is to move slowly and steadily.

- Allow your scroll saw to do its work because, unlike other saws, this one is quite independent. It powers the force that drives the blade with its motor, and so, all you have to do is guide the outline of your design to the side of the moving saw blade.

P.S: Never press the wooden plaque to the blade. Just see that it moves through your design smoothly and nicely.

- Did you know that you could cut through several wooden plaques at a time? Yes! As long as the wooden plaques are of the same size and have the same design, you could stack them along with each other and then keep them that way. Repeating a cut for each plaque can be very annoying and tiring, and as you go on, you'd even notice that your project's rougher around the edges since you'll feel completely stressed out towards the end.

  So, bind the multiple pieces together with a tape whose color contrasts with that of the wood for clarity's sake.

- To increase the lifespan of your blades, use WD-40 on them. When you are done using your scroll saw, remove the clamp's blade and then spray it thinly with the WD-40. It will prevent the blades from getting rusted on exposure to air or moisture. And if your blade doesn't get rusted, it comes out stronger and lives longer.

  However, if you can't lay your hands on WD-40, you could work with oil instead. Just rub it thinly around the blade.

Chapter 3

Getting Started with Scroll Saw

Basic Scroll Saw Tools and Supplies

We will now look at the various tools that will help you when working with a scroll saw.

Wood

Getting the right wood is very important in your scroll saw project. It is this exact supply that will determine how your project will look like at the end. We will go through a few things you should consider when choosing the wood to use for your project, the various types of wood available out there, and whether you should use them or not.

But before then, a few points to take note of.

- You will know if a particular wood plaque is good when it doesn't break or dent your saw blade.
- You can exercise more control with thin materials.

- Hardwood will increase the vibration you encounter while working with your scroll saw because they offer high resistance levels to every physical property that hits them. However, hardwoods can hold the patterns cut on them better.

- You should also consider the fact that scroll saw works best on thin materials and that the highest density of wood a scroll saw blade could cut through is the one that is two inches deep. Any material that is denser than two inches will destroy your blade.

- If you are using hardwood, you will have to work slowly to prevent your blade from snapping into two.

- Thinner wood plaques will offer little to no resistance to the vibration that hits them, and this can cause issues with you cutting along with the outline of the design you already prepared.

- For practical sessions as a beginner, start with softwood. They are easy to work through as they easily part under the influence of the blade. They may not hold in the patterns well enough, but then, you can end up with great practice projects.

Later, as you get better, you can proceed to use hardwood.

- Hardwoods will offer a lot of resilience, so if you run the blade quickly through them, you might end up burning the wood or chipping it. Beginners should stay away from hardwood as they require some level of skills when working with them.

Once you have made the considerations outlined above, you can now move on to the next part about the different types of wood you will find in the store, as given below.

Pine

Pine is one wood you should try to stay away from when doing your scroll saw projects. Even though it is relatively cheap, it has different grain colors. One is light, and one is dark, with each offering different degrees of resistance. To work with Pine, nevertheless, you'd have to change your blades intermittently to meet the resistance each grain layer will offer, and this can be very time-wasting. Projects done with Pine are mostly of very low quality, and you'd not want that after all of the stress you have put into your work.

Poplar wood

Poplar is a better choice when compared to Pine for your wood projects. Poplar wood has a regular grain pattern that the saw blade can run through easily and smoothly without facing any form of resistance. It also has a light tone that will make your cuttings nice to look at. You can also get Poplar wood easily from the wood stores near you.

Plywood

Plywood is really good for scroll saw projects. It has a high tensile strength that can hold in your cuttings. It is also very stable, even with all the vibration you might encounter when using the scroll saw. However, plywood weakens saw blades very quickly as opposed to soft solid wood.

Walnut

Walnut has a dark color tone that can be very useful if you create dark cuttings. They have a lot of grain lines and are relatively permeable to the moving blade. The sapwood for walnut is white. Walnut is cheap to get though and is readily available. Walnut is not as strong as Maple or Birch, but then, it is tougher than Cherry.

Cherry

Cherry is a block of dark wood with pale streaks of wood, breaking its color tone's uniformity. This particular attribute can be nice for projects that need various patterns and designs. It also has minimal sapwood of a reddish-yellow hue. Cherry darkens when exposed to sunlight, and it also gets distorted as it dries.

Red oak

Red oak is a hardwood that has a whole lot of grains. This makes it suitable for your scroll saw projects. However, it would be best if you were careful not to quickly run the blades through the wood to prevent it from burning or chipping. The slow speed will also help your blades to last long. So, before you make big designs on red oak, make sure you do several practical sessions on red oak scraps.

Hickory

This hardwood has no resin. It also has a very prominent grain pattern. The color tone is so dark that you'd love it for your dark projects. It is also a very cheap hardwood with great strength to weight ratio that is wonderful for holding in your cuts.

Polywood

Polywood is a kind of wood that has been around for a time as long as the 90s. However, it has undergone several modifications that have made it better over the years. Plywood was produced from polyethylene thermoplastics and other recycled materials. These components make the wood resistant to adverse weather conditions and water. It is also friendly to the environment as it was made from recycled materials like plastic. If your scroll saw is going to be displayed outside, you might want to use this wood.

Maple

This is one hardwood with a color tone that is lighter than Cherry or Walnut. Maple also has an even grain that won't obstruct the fluid movement of your blade. So, you can work with this for your scroll saw projects.

Birch

Birch is a hardwood that has little to no sapwood. Its heart is of a creamy white color with a curly and distinctive grain. It is just like Maple when their degrees of toughness are closely compared to each other. Birch has an even color tone that makes it very suitable for your scroll saw projects. The grains of this wood will also take in stains more readily.

Ashwood

Ashwood can be very tough on the scroll saw blades, and so, you suffer from the issue of dented or broken blades if you go too fast. It also has fine grain lines that can add a lot of beauty to your projects and, at the same time, offer you a lot of complications when dealing with a project that involves you making several intricate designs and curves.

So, generally, when choosing your wood, go for something that allows you to make several intricate turns and details. Hardwoods are still the best for scroll saw projects because they offer more resistance when the blade tries to make several curves and turns. You should also choose wood whose density can be handled by the blade you have.

Scroll Saw

The scroll saw is the device that you use for the cutting itself. It is usually fixed and has many components that will aid you when doing your scroll saw projects. The blade is usually powered by electricity or mechanical pedaling.

Components of a Scroll Saw

A beginner's scroll saw machine must have at least all of the following parts.

1. **The power button**: This is the button you flip or press to get the blade of your scroll saw moving. This button will be very handy when the blade breaks and won't stop moving until the motor is stopped. And trust me, broken saw blades are very common with scroll saws. Make sure the switch is one that isn't below the saw or under the worktable.

2. **The speed button:** This button either increases or decreases the speed of the blade. You need to put it at the back of your mind that you'll be working with all kinds of materials, and each one can be operated upon at a particular speed. First, as a beginner, you might need to start at low speeds and later proceed to faster speeds. This reason is

why you should ensure that your device has this button.

3. **The table:** This is a platform where you lay the wood you plan to use for your project.

4. **Blade guard:** This component will prevent your fingers from slipping towards the moving blade.

5. **The tilt lock knob:** This knob helps you adjust the table's height or tilt the table to a comfortable angle for you to operate from. This way, you can make neater cuts on the wooden plaque.

6. **Blade tension knob:** This knob will help you to adjust the tension of the blade. You might have to use this knob every time you need to work with your scroll saw.

7. **Blade clamps:** This holds the blade in place and prevents it from moving about or slipping while it moves through the wood. There is one clamp at the upper part of the table that's fixed to the arm. There's also another one that is fixed to the bottom of the table.

8. **Dust blower:** This prevents dust from accumulating on the surface of your project by blowing it off at regular intervals.

Scroll Saw Adhesives

The adhesive you use for your scroll saw projects depends on how soft the wood is. Before fixing the outline to the wood, make sure the wood's surface is plane and smooth. You should also remove any sawdust that could have accumulated on the surface by rubbing it with a dry cloth. The other smaller dust particles can be gotten rid of by running your palm lightly across the surface.

When working with softwood, you can use adhesives like painter's tape, Elmer's glue spray, graphite or carbon paper, or sticky labels. Using stronger glues like the temporary-bond adhesive spray and the clear packaging tape on softwood can end up chipping the wood as you tear off the outline from its surface. And chipped wood plaques can result in the waste of hours and energy spent on the project.

Let's look at a few adhesives and see the kind of wood they work best on.

- **The temporary-bond spray adhesive**

The temporary-bond adhesive has several types. Some of them are gentle, and the others are harsh. Some artists go for mild ones like Elmer's glue or glue sticks. The other artists work with stronger adhesives like the 3M adhesive or Loctite.

Fixing a design to the surface of the wood plaque for your project

You can fix it directly to the wood surface. To do this, follow the procedures below:

1. Hold the edges of the design's outline straight up in the air to stretch it out evenly.
2. Spray the backside of the outline with the glue. If the glue is thick enough, one spray should do the trick. However, if it isn't, you may have to cover it two to three times with the glue aerosol.
3. Wait for the glue you sprayed at the back of the design to get sticky. This procedure should happen in less than a minute.
4. Fix the sticky outline to the wood's surface while making sure to apply it slowly, inch after inch.

5. Spread your fingers across the surface of the outline to eradicate the air bubbles that might have formed underneath it.
6. Wait for a few minutes for the outline to dry. The time for the drying varies with the humidity and temperature of your workroom.

The cheaper options of the temporary-bond adhesives are Elmer's glue, etc. The grip of this offer may not be as strong as the one offered by the former. The bad thing that could occur along the way is the outline coming off the wood's surface even while cutting with your scroll saw. Using adhesives like clear packaging tape or the painter's masking tape can be better, cheaper options.

Advantages of using the temporary-bond adhesive spray

1. You can finish applying this to the back of the design in no time.
2. This glue dries quickly.
3. It can be applied evenly across the surface.

What are the disadvantages?

1. Because of the strength of this glue, you may end up pulling out the wood fibers if you apply too much of it on softwood.
2. In a case where the design you glued to the wooden surface takes days to complete, you might end up having issues removing it.
3. There could be a residue of the design even after pulling the main outline off. To remove that residue, you might have to use an adhesive remover like alcohol or paint thinner.
4. You can only use this glue in a place with cross-ventilation.

- **Clear Packaging Tape**

This tape is also known as masking tape. With this, you don't have to deal with the issue of having residual design outlines after you have peeled the major design off. To use this tape, you could fix the tape to the wood's surface and then place the design's outline on it.

The clear packaging tape should only be used on hardwoods because if they are left on softwoods' surfaces for a long time, the fibers could end up getting chipped depending on how strong the glue is. Another issue that could arise from using this method is the time it takes to make the tape layers even. The tape must also not come on top of each other or have spaces between them as it could cause the design's surface to be uneven. Making sure of this can be very stressful and time-consuming.

Advantages

1. You can peel off the design outline and have little to no residual of the outline after. It all depends on how long you leave your design on the wooden surface.
2. This style is wonderful for cutting through hardwoods.
3. The tape's glue can help reduce the friction your wood feeds to the blade while cutting through it.
4. With this method, you can also begin to stain the wood right after cutting through it. This advantage is because the tape dries quickly.

Disadvantages

1. When using this tape on softwood, make sure that it does not remain on the surface for more than three days.

2. Laying the strips of tape can be very time-consuming.
3. If the tape overlaps, there could be issues related to the design's creasing or cutting problems.

- **Painter's Masking Tape**

The adhesive behind this tape is not as strong as the ones listed above. So, if you peel it off the wood, there's a lesser possibility of the wood fibers being chipped off in the process. The artists arrange the strips of tape across the wooden surface to use it and then fix the design's outline on the interconnected tapes.

Advantages

1. When you peel the design from the wooden surface, you will have little to no residue on the surface.
2. This tape is great for any wood.
3. Even if this tape is left on the wood surface for days, there is a very low possibility that the fibers will be pulled out as you rip off the design.
4. The glue from the tape reduces friction as the blade moves through the wood.

5. Immediately after cutting the wood, you can start staining.

Disadvantages

1. Arranging the layers of tape on the surface may take longer.
2. There could be a risk of creases when cutting through the wood.

- **Clear Laminating or Shelving paper**

This paper is also known as the contact paper. It is not a common adhesive. It is a transparent piece of plastic that has a side covered with glue. To use this, fix the shelving paper on the wooden surface and then place the design on it.

Advantages.

1. It is simpler to use in comparison to the tape.
2. There is little to no residue left on the wooden surface after the design has been ripped off.
3. It is just as cheap as the tape.
4. There is no risk of overlapping since this adhesive does not work with strips of glue

Disadvantages.

1. Applying this sheet could take a lot of time.

- **Large Labels**

This particular adhesive involves the art of fixing design outlines to the side of sticky labels. All you have to do is get a sticky label with no design and then print your design on it with any printing device.

Advantages.

1. This is a clean and fast method.
2. There is no issue of wrong and unbalanced layers or creasing.
3. The label can be removed easily after cutting.

Disadvantages.

1. You will need a printer to make the labels.

To peel off the adhesives, you can use either of the following options.

1. Mineral Spirit

If you have any residual design outlines still stuck to the wood after peeling it off, this adhesive can help achieve that purpose. Just get a piece of cloth, soak it with the mineral spirit and then, dab it across the design outline. Let the paper absorb it for a period close to twenty seconds. After this period, the paper should come off easily on its own. In case you don't want something with a strong smell, you can go for the practically odorless mineral spirit.

2. Adhesive Removers

This one combines removing agents like acetone and paint thinners. Adhesive removers are also used in a manner that's similar to the way mineral spirits are used.

3. Sanding

This method of removing adhesives cab be effective only when you have little residue left. Sanding will also be the best thing for you to do if you need to stain your design immediately after cutting. This process also does not take time.

Clamps

Clamps help to hold on to the blade of your scroll saw. It will help you avoid issues in which the blade slips while you are cutting wood. Most problems occur with the upper clamp of a scroll saw machine, and it's for two reasons.

1. The clamp's insides could become smooth, so there is no opposition to the blade's movement. Once the screws become weak, the blade slips right out of the clamp.
2. The presence of oil in the interior linings could cause the blade to slip out of its hold. This oil is usually caused by the oils that line the blades. The oil mostly prevents the blade from rusting, but it causes the clamp to wear out prematurely.

To make your clamp better, you can use sandpaper to roughen the insides a bit so that the tripping can be better. You can also reduce the blade's oil's adverse effects on the clamp by cleaning the part that goes into the clamp with alcohol.

Drill Bits

The blades of the scroll saw exist in different sizes, widths, and tip settings. They are used to scroll in different kinds of patterns into wood. For instance, if you want to scroll in extremely detailed wood points, you could use very narrow blades with bigger drill bits. The drill bits usually occur at the end of the blade.

Types of drill bits

1. Hand drill
2. Drill press

The drill press is a kind of drill bit that makes neater and very real drills in wood quickly. The spindle can be set to 1600 revolutions per minute, which is quite suitable for softwood, or 3000 revolutions per minute, suitable for hardwoods. You could also easily switch to the other intermediate speeds while cutting through wood plaques.

For wood that is about ¼ to ½ inches thick, i.e., for thin wooden plaques, you could use hand drills. If the wood density is more than that, a drill press will be more than suitable for it. The drill press will drill holes that are straight down and neat. The most commonly used drill size is a one-sixteenth inch bit. If you want to vein your wood, you could use extremely smaller ones like one-sixty-fourth inch bit. However, you might need special clamps to hold these kinds of bits.

The drill bits of a saw are there to help you make very accurate and quick cuts into the wood. Also, saws that make use of painless blades often are the best as they are very suitable for cutting interior angles that require high levels of intricacy. Pinned blades are thick and wide, unsuitable for such intricate details. Now, this kind of blade would never really size a hole drilled by a small drill bit.

Scroll Saw Blades—Choosing the Right Blades

The blade of scroll saws can either have a plain end or a pin end. As a beginner, you should choose a scroll saw that works with either of the blades. Blades with pin-ends cannot make cuttings in the interior parts of your scroll saw project. You can only use it for exterior designs, though. Pinned blades are usually too thick and wide for small holes drilled into wood and cannot make interior designs. Pinless saws, however, are the best as they make intricate and inner designs.

Things to look out for when choosing the right blade

1. How thick is the wood you plan on using for your project? The denser the wood you want to use, the bigger the blade you should use. To know how big a blade is, you can check its grade number. Blades with grade numbers like five and seven are usually big.

2. How hard is the material you are using? Hardwoods like cherry and Walnut require blades with big teeth to cut through them. You could use the grade 5 or grade 7 blades if the wood is about ¾ inches thick. For anything thicker than that, use blades higher than grade 9. These blades are usually not prone to breaking when you apply pressure to them. They also cut through hardwood real quick.

   For thin wood, use blades of smaller grades. Thin plaques of wood are usually subject to a lot of vibration since they have little to no resistance, so using a small blade will only be to your advantage.

   When cutting through a pile of wooden plaques, work with a blade whose grade can handle the overall thickness. For example, if you are working on cutting through eight plaques where each has a density of ⅛ inches, you ought to work with a blade of grade number five or seven.

3. How complex is the project you are working on? Patterns that have a lot of complexities and intricate patterns require a blade with small teeth.

Large blades cannot cut through tight edges and corners. To get a quality result with a project involving many intricacies, it would be best to go for blades with small sizes.

Types of scroll saw blades

1. **Standard tooth blade:** This is an entire saw blade in which all the teeth are the same distance away from each other. The two types of standard tool blades available are wooden blades and metal blades. Wooden blades have bigger teeth with a lot of space in between the teeth. Wooden blades will also help you take the sawdust off the wooden surface. Metal blades have teeth of smaller proportion and little space in between the teeth.

2. **Skip tooth blade:** Skip tooth blades have portions on the blade with no teeth, i.e., missing tooth. This will make your cutting procedures slow as lesser teeth are moving through the wood. As a beginner, you should go for this kind of blade.

3. **Double tooth blade:** In this kind of blade, you will find so much space between two sets of teeth.

Also, because there are lesser teeth, the cutting procedures will take longer. Although, you can be sure of getting an even cut.

4. **Reverse tooth blade:** This blade looks exactly like the skip tooth blade. However, the teeth that exist at the end of the blade don't project downwards. Instead, their rings pile upwards. Reverse tooth blades are great if you want to avoid having splintered wood. When fixing this blade to the clamp, ensure that it is set so that only two or three of the teeth project are above the saw arm when the table is at the highest it can be.

5. **Precision ground tooth blade:** The teeth in this blade are smaller than those in a skip tooth blade. The teeth also have a unique appearance as they appear to blend with the other parts of the blade with no teeth. You can use this kind of blade to cut straight lines through your wooden plaque.

   P.S: Beginners should stay away from the Precision round tooth blade. This note is because using the blade requires the crafter having a particular level of skill first.

6. **Spiral blades:** These kinds of blades are completely covered with teeth across all their lengths. With this blade, if you want to cut through ninety or greater angles, you don't have to push the blade back and then start turning the wood around. You could use this blade to cut through any direction without having to pause to slit the wood. Spiral cuts make rough cuts and require a little bit of expertise before they can be used effectively.

7. **Crown tooth blades:** This is the blade that is recently used in the world of craft. While one tooth of the crown-tooth blade cuts in one direction, the adjacent tooth will cut in the opposite direction.

Scroll Saw Basics

- **Squaring the Table**

The adjustable table of scroll saws enables the device to be easily inclined or declined to any angle. Some cuttings can only be made when the table has deviated from its plane axis, i.e., when it is at an angle to the horizontal. This technique is important for executing several projects like intarsia and puzzle pieces since they have a lot of angles that must be cut delicately.

To square a table, one could work with a small metallic square or a right-angled tool.

How do you square a table?

1. All you need to do is position the metallic square against the ridges of the blade.

   P.S: Make sure the blade has been clamped down and tensioned rightly.

2. Alter the angle at which the table is to the blade. Make sure you shift it until it is exactly at 90° to it.

Another method of squaring a table is by cutting through a scrap wood block that is at least ¾ inches thick. When you are done, you can then check for the angle at which the cut was made using the metallic square. Alter until you get a perfect square; keep on altering the angle the table is at to the horizontal axis.

The Kerf test method involves getting a ¾ inches thick piece of scrap wood and then cutting through a depth of ½ inches through it. Once you are done with that, power off the scroll saw device and move the blade out. If the blade easily settles in the Kerf, it means the table is square enough. However, if the blade does not slip into the Kerf, repeat the procedures above until it does.

- **Fixing Design Outlines**

When fixing the design's outline to the surface of a wooden plaque, most artists have used the temporary bond spray adhesives, and some others used strong adhesives like Elmer's glue. Adhesives like masking tapes will help a lot to lubricate the blade. Also, the design's outline can be easily removed later.

To work with an adhesive, follow the procedures below;

1. Make a photocopied outline of the intended design.

2. Spray the aerosol of the adhesive to the back of the design outline.
3. Wait for about thirty seconds for the glue to become relatively sticky.
4. Fix the sticky outline on the pretty-arranged layers of tape strips.

If you used either the rubber cement adhesive or the cement glue, you'd still use it the same way. Shelf paper is a plastic adhesive that most artists prefer to use. Place the shelf paper to the wood's surface and make sure that the shiny side faces you. The next thing is for you to cut spray the back of the design with an adhesive. After waiting for a few seconds, place the design outline on that shiny part of the shelf paper. To finally fix the sheets to the board, peel off the lining at the shelf paper's back to expose the sticky side.

Graphite or carbon paper is another option. Fix one edge of your design outline to the board with clear tape and then, slip a sheet of carbon or graphite paper between the sheet and the board through the other edge. When you are done, you can tape the other end finally. The next thing to do is to use a transfer tip to run through the design outlines. If you are working with a block of dark wood like Alder, make sure you work with graphite or carbon sheets with light backs. The difference between graphite and carbon paper is that the latter is cheaper. However, before you can get rid of the outlines it made on the wood, you may have to run sandpaper across the surface.

- **Stack Cutting**

With this cutting method, you can cut through several wood plaques simultaneously as long as they have the same design. To do this, fix many of the plaques together and then cut through them as if you are cutting through one piece of wood.

You can attach the wooden plaques with tapes. All you need to do is pile up the layers and then allow the blade of your scroll saw to cut through them as one. To keep the plaques stable and in place, run a long piece of adhesive tape around the sides. You could either use masking tape, painter's tape, or clear packaging tape. Hotly melted glue will also do the trick. Just apply dots of it at the wooden plaques' edges and then press them firmly together.

Another technique you can work with is driving nails through the edges of the wooden plaques or driving brads that will keep the wooden pieces together.

- **Blade Tension**

To check for the tension in your blade, ensure that the clamps and blade holders tightly grip both the blade's edges. Next, you can use your forefinger to push at the middle of the blade slightly. A blade under the right amount of tension will not shift more than ⅛ inches forward, backward, or to any other side.

If a blade isn't under the right tension, you will notice it wandering about under your finger's push. Apart from that, the blade will make several irregular, rough, and wagging cuts that will only ruin your project. However, take note that you shouldn't press too hard on a loosely tensioned blade. Doing that will only cause it to snap into two. A blade under too many tensional forces will break and could even pull out of the blade holders. Generally, please make the blade tighter than it is loose.

- **Blade-entry Holes**

To make some designs, especially the interior ones, you may drill a hole through the top panels first. When drilling the hole, make sure it is in a direction that is perpendicular to the wooden plaque. To make these holes, you could use a hand drill. This drill will help you to make the holes as vertical as possible. To prevent the wood from chipping by the sides or at the back, use a bigger bit. Narrow blades can be easily passed through bigger bits. To make thin veining cuts, you will have to work with the smallest bit you can find.

- **Removing Design Outlines**

Paper outlines can be removed by running a towel that has been pre-soaked into mineral spirits or adhesive removers through the wood.

- **Photocopying Design Outlines**

When photocopying patterns, it is better to use the same machine to make copies of all the projects. This will help prevent the designs from being distorted, especially in cases where the design is huge. You can also be sure that the patterns head in the same direction.

Finishing Your Scroll Saw Project

Rather than leaving your project in its wooden state, you could apply finishes to make them come out more beautiful and exquisite. Also, if your project was designed for exterior display, there could be a situation where dust accumulates on the surface. If the project were finished, wiping that dust off would be much easier. Finishes work to shield the intricacy of projects, and the degree to which these finishes shield projects vary from one to the other. Lastly, finishes will help your project's natural color and grains to be the main thing. So, it can be inferred that finishes work to protect and enhance the beauty of a project.

However, finishes cannot just be used on any wooden surface. There's a particular level of preparation that must be attained before you can go on using any finish. The preparation that must first be done is the sanding process. Sanding the wood before you begin a project will help to minimize to a large extent the amount of sanding you have to do at the end.

For sanding a plaque of wood, you could either use your hand or other sanding tools. Sanding with your hand is best for small projects. You could wrap it around a box so you can cover more areas in a little time. For larger projects that require a level and flat surface, you could either use a palm sander or an orbital sander. Sanding only makes the surface of your wood as smooth as its pores can generally take. So, yes, you could sand the surface of the wood to the point that no other sandpaper, no matter how small the grit is, will be able to further smoothen the wood's surface.

When you are sanding a wooden plaque, run the sandpaper in the direction of the wood's grains. Start with the sandpaper with the roughest grits, i.e., one with 80-grits. Then, you could later proceed to ones with smoother grits like 150-grits. The larger the grits, the smoother the sandpaper is. You could find sandpaper of grits as high as 700 grits.

As you change the sandpapers to higher grits, make sure you wipe off the dust before moving to the next grit of sandpaper. For this, you could use a lint-free cloth that will catch every microscopic speck of sawdust or a largely squared paintbrush with hard bristles.

Now, the next step involves you applying varnishes like Danish oil, Tung oil, lemon oil, or boiled linseed oil to the surface of the wood. These oils are finishers that help your project to stand the test of time. This, however, is unnecessary if you plan on applying layers of paint to your woodwork project later on. You could also use furniture wax liquid that can deeply permeate the fibers of the wood. Use an artist's brush of the medium size to apply the furniture wax to the design's inner parts. If the project is small enough, you could immerse the whole structure into the wax liquid to cover every part of it. To get rid of the excess finish varnish, you could use a lint-free cloth. After, allow the varnish on the small piece to dry. Shortly after, you will notice how the original grain and color tone of the wood became even more prominent. This is because the oil wax gets rid of the sawdust swallowed up by the wooden fibers.

Spray varnishes and lacquers exist in several forms like gloss, semi-gloss, and satin finishes. After spraying the wooden surface with one coat of the spray varnish, you'd notice that the grains on the wood become even more prominent and raised. The degree to which the wood gets raised depends heavily on the kind of varnish you use and the kind of wood you lay your patterns. When the varnish is completely dried, you can use a fine sandpaper-like one with 220 grits or 280 grits to polish the surface. Make sure you run the sandpaper in the direction of the grains of the wood.

Note:

1. While working with spray varnishes, ensure that you wear a nose mask to protect your lungs from the concentrated fumes.
2. You should also work in a place with cross-ventilation.

3. To get the varnish on a wooden surface to dry quickly, make sure that you work in a place with plenty of sunlight.
4. Before you spray any varnish on your wooden surface, make sure that you must have wiped the surface with a lint-free cloth to get rid of the dust on it. You surely wouldn't want to see dust particles sticking themselves to the varnish.

You can also decide to work with liquid varnishes rather than the ones in the form of aerosols. The only issue with liquid varnishes is the fact that they take longer hours to get dried. There is also no way to cut through the long wait. To apply this varnish to a woodwork project, get a painter's brush, dip it in the varnish, and then brush it across the wood's surface.

Vanishes dry through a series of chemical reactions while lacquer dries with the concept of solvent evaporation. There are many types of lacquers, and a few of them include; alkyd, polyurethane, spar, etc.

Alkyds take a very long time to dry, and when they eventually do, they develop a warm color and a hard coat of finish.

Polyurethane dries faster than alkyds do, and their finish is usually harder than the one alkyds have to offer. The color, however, is not as mellow as the ones alkyds have. If you used this finish, your project would come out with an unparalleled shine.

Spar lacquer works best for coating the surfaces of outdoor projects as it has a soft finish. It also takes a very long time to dry off completely, and when it does, eventually, it comes off with an amber color. Spar lacquer also contains some ultraviolet inhibitors that protect your project from the harsh influence of the sun. Water-based varnishes include gel varnishes. The kind of finish you eventually work with will be determined by how durable you want the project to be. Also, the way you want the project to look eventually also determines a whole lot of things.

To use paint-on finishes, go through the instructions provided by the manufacturer first. As you apply the finishes in layers, use the sandpaper between each layer to smoothen the surfaces. For woods like oak, you may need three layers of coating to finish coating the project.

To use a wood stain on a project before working with either a varnish or lacquer finish, wait for the paint to dry off first. Then, from there, you can follow the steps already outlined above to complete the procedure.

Scroll Saw Safety Procedures

1. To prevent sawdust particles from entering your eyes, make sure that you wear your safety glasses at all times.
2. Cover your toes and feet with shoes or boots made from thick leather.
3. Remove rings and jewelry from your fingers before working on your scroll saw the device.
4. If you have long hair that is always down, make sure you pack it up into a ponytail or bun to ensure that the strands don't disturb your vision as you work.
5. Do not wear baggy clothes while working! Stick with tight-fitting clothes that won't have you taking time to adjust falling sleeves or collars.
6. You might need ear muffs if you know your ears cannot handle the sound of the hurting machine and moving blade.
7. Your scroll saw must be fixed onto a regular and stable surface. This will help you get very accurate cuts.

8. Plug your scroll saw device into an available socket that will provide a stable electricity supply.

9. Mark off the areas you use for working and make sure that you have a safety kit within your workspace and passageway in case of emergencies.

10. Before turning on your scroll, see the device and make sure that the blade's clamp is in position.

11. Choose the right size and style of a blade that will work best for your wood before powering on your scroll saw device. This is where you need to consider your options. Are you working with hard or softwood? Are you making intricate and interior designs? Are you going to make several bends as you cut?

12. The teeth of the blade you use for cutting through the wood must project downwards towards the table's level surface.

13. Tighten the clamps around the blade at the top and the bottom, and then make sure that it aligns with the blade support.

14. Do not work with a faulty scroll saw machine.

15. Keep all of your fingers away from the path your blade runs through.

16. If you are working with small-sized pieces of wood, do not hold them with your hands because there's a strong possibility of your fingers finding their way to the blade's guard unknowingly. So, instead, you could use a pair of forceps or jigs to hold the wood in place.

17. Ensure that there are no nails on the surface of the wood you want to cut on.

18. Clear off foreign objects from your work surface and tables.

19. Set the 'hold down foot' so that it just touches the surface of the wood lightly.

20. Before you begin work with your scroll saw, make sure that you start the dust blower first.

21. Observe how the blade moves first before proceeding to cut your wood with it. If the blade makes a strange noise or quivers too much, stop the scroll saw at once. Power off the device and then isolate it until you can detect and correct the problem.

22. Before you start working with the blade of your saw, allow it to run until it reaches the speed at which it is highly functional.

23. Do not force the wooden plaque towards the blade. Just guide it slowly towards the blade and let it cut through the wood at its pace.

24. When guiding the wood towards the blade, use your fingers and thumb. The other thumb should be raised so that your whole fingers don't just slip right into the blade.

25. When working, keep your face to the side of the saw while making sure that you aren't facing the blade's line. That line is the path a broken blade will follow, and that can be fatal if it pierces your skin.

26. Before you go ahead to take away scraps from the surface of your wood or to adjust anything, make sure that the scroll saw has been turned off first and that the blade has completely stopped running.

27. Never reach under the table for anything while the saw is powered on.

28. When cutting with your scroll saw, make sure you give it your full attention.

29. When cutting through tight corners, use relief cuts.

30. Ensure that a cylindrical wood is cut with a miter gauge so that it doesn't roll out of your hands at any time.

31. Before you get rid of the waste materials that have settled on the surface of the wood you are working on, make sure that you wait for the blade to stop running entirely.

32. Do not try to run the scroll saw faster than it ought to move; otherwise, you may end up losing control and then have your fingers slip towards the moving blade.

33. Before cutting out any great wood designs, make sure you have run several practice tests on some scrap piece of wood first.

34. Ensure that all the guards in your scroll saw device is set to a closed fix before storing your scroll saw away.

35. Always store the machine in a cool, dry, and tidy place where dust or water cannot find its way through.

A Short message from the Author:

Hey, I hope you are enjoying the book? I would love to hear your thoughts!

Many readers do not know how hard reviews are to come by and how much they help an author.

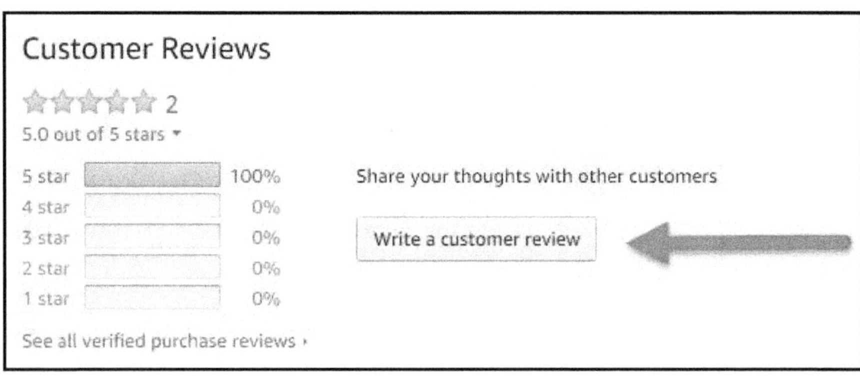

I would be incredibly grateful if you could take just 60 seconds to write a short review on Amazon, even if it is a few sentences!

>> Click here to leave a quick review

Thanks for the time taken to share your thoughts!

Chapter 4

Scroll Saw Project Ideas

Now that you know how the scroll saw works and its other essential components, let's go through some of the excellent projects you can get started with right away. Even though they are beginner-friendly, you still need to exercise a lot of patience as you execute them.

When you are done with each project, take time to study the sides, and see if there are any bumps or irregularities along the lines. To help yourself get better, repeat each project you aren't satisfied with until you get the best result. The whole thing gets more interesting as you proceed. At some point, you might even be able to cut through woods without having a design pressed to the wood.

Cat

This design will help you practice how to cut through curves.

Materials

- ¾" by 4½" by 5½" pinewood.
- Temporary bond spray adhesive or glue stick.

- Grade 5 skip-tooth blade.
- Adhesive remover or Mineral Spirit.

Procedures

1. Make a clear photocopied outline of a cat.

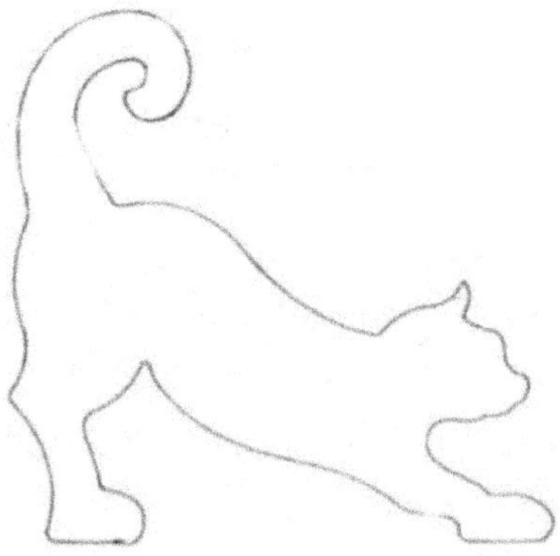

2. Spray the temporary bond spray adhesive along the back of the outline. Do not spray the wood! That can make the removal of the patterns very difficult.
3. Fix the outline centrally to the surface of the pinewood.
4. Ensure that your wooden plaque has a dimension that is ¼ inches larger than the actual design so that it will fit. The dimension of wood you saw in

the material section is perfect enough to give you corners you can hold on to as you work.

5. Insert the blade into the blade clamps while making sure that the teeth are projecting downwards. You should also check the blade's tension to ensure that it isn't too stiff or too loose. If it is under the right tension force, you will hear a ping sound when the blade is plucked.

6. The blade must be at an angle of 90° to the saw. You can use a metallic square to do this.

7. Turn on your scroll saw device.

8. Place your fingers at the edges and slowly guide the pinewood to the moving blade.

9. If you miss the line, do not try to force the blade back to the side to get back to the sides you missed. Just continue by steering back gradually to the rest lines. Keep your shoulders relaxed; it's just a cutting procedure, nothing much.

10. When you approach the parts with curves, fluidly turn your wooden plaque so that the blade can cut it roundly. This is different from the 'cross' project because you don't need straight edges.

11. When you get to the heels of the cat, bend the pinewood sharply so that the blade cuts something very similar to the apex of the triangle.
12. When you are done cutting out the outlines, turn off the scroll saw.
13. The outline of the cat will then drop out of the major wooden plaque.
14. Dab the surface of the cat with the outlines with a towel soaked in mineral spirit. Then, wait for about half a minute for the paper to come undone.
15. You are done!

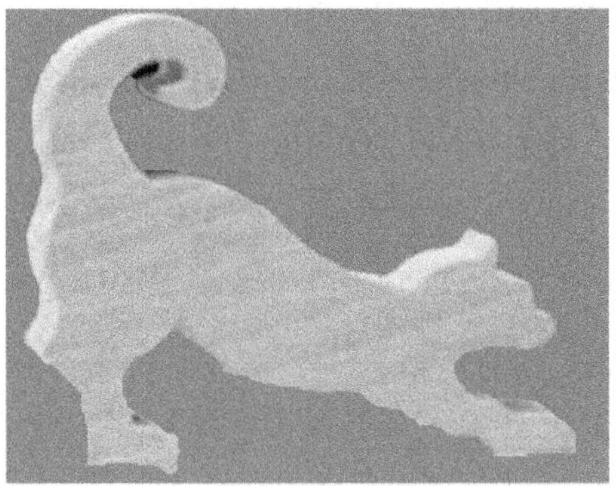

Maple Leaf

This design will teach you how to cut out sharp corners.

Materials

- Scroll saw device.
- ¾" by 3½" by 3½" of pinewood.
- Temporary bond spray adhesive.
- Grade 5 skip-tooth blade.
- Mineral spirit or Adhesive remover.

Procedures

1. Make a photocopy of the design of a maple leaf and make sure the outlines are in clear black prints.

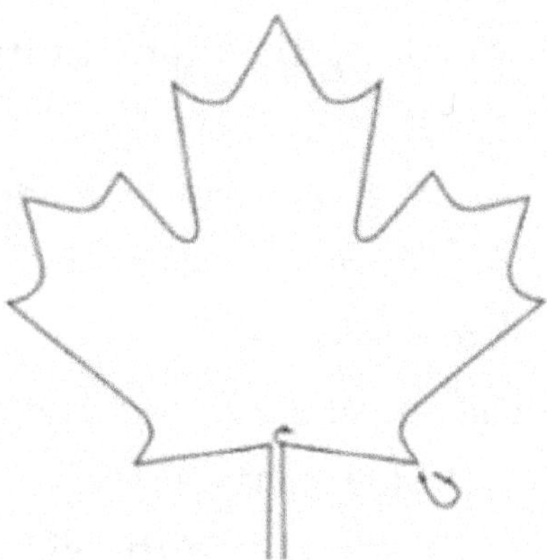

2. Spray the temporary bond adhesive remover at the back of the outline and then wait for it to become sticky.

P.S: Make sure that you do not spray this adhesive on the wood. If you spray it at the back of the design's outline instead, you can make sure that the glue does not penetrate the fibers of the wood. This way, the future stains or finishes you might make won't get affected by the glue.

3. Attach the sticky design outline to the surface of the pinewood.
4. Ensure that the size of the wood you use is almost the same as the length of the borders for your maple leaf's outline.
5. Insert the blade within its clamp. Check for the tension by plucking the blade at its center and if it makes the ping sound, continue by ensuring that the teeth of the blade projects downwards. You should also make sure that the blade is at an angle of 90° to the wood.
6. Power on the scroll saw machine and wait for the blade to run at its normal speed.
7. Gently press the wood to the side of the running blade. Place your fingers by the corners and begin to push it towards the blade.
8. Start cutting from the stalk of the maple leaf before proceeding to make those sharp cuts and

turns. The first sharp corner you will approach is the junction between the stalk of the leaf and the leaf.

9. To make a sharp turn, stop pushing the wood for a while before you turn the wood sharply as you approach those areas so that the blade cuts that way too.

10. Cut through the second corner, too, the same way you did with the first corner. However, when you approach the next sharp edge, which is the lower end of the leaf, use the loop method to create a sharp point. This loop method involves you cutting beyond the design lines and then looping back around as you begin to cut through the pre-set lines. Use this loop procedure to cut the other sharp edges of your design.

11. When you are done with the outlines, turn off the engine of the scroll saw device.

12. Dab the surface of the outline with mineral spirit to weaken the glue and then, wait for about thirty seconds before pulling off the sheet of paper.

13. You are done!

Bell

Materials

- A scroll saw machine.
- ¾ inches thick pine wood.
- Temporary bond spray adhesive or glue sticks.
- Grade 5 skip tooth blade.
- Adhesive remover.

Procedures

1. Make a clear and neat photocopy of the outline of a bell. The outline has to be in clear and bold black lines.

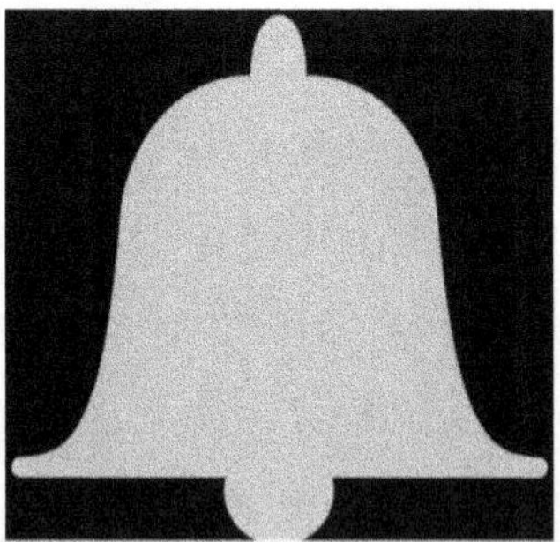

2. Spray the temporary bond spray adhesive at the back of the paper holding the adhesive. Then,

wait for some time (about thirty seconds) for the glue in it to get activated.

3. Press the outline to the surface of your pinewood.
4. Run your palm across the surface of the outline to eradicate the air spaces beneath it.
5. Wait for a few seconds for the paper to get properly fixed to the pinewood.
6. Now, before you turn on the scroll saw machine, check the blade's teeth and make sure they are projecting downwards. To check for the blade's tension, use the tip of your finger to press against the middle of the blade. It must not shift more than $\frac{1}{8}$ inches to any side. You could also pluck it and wait to hear the ping sound.
7. Adjust the tension of the blade if necessary.
8. Position your blade so that it points towards the tip of the bell.
9. You can now turn on the saw.
10. Place your two hands on the pinewood and guide it gently towards the running blade. Make sure you don't press in on it too hard or force it on the blade. You should also ensure that your arms and shoulders are not tensed as you guide the pinewood towards the blade.

11. Guide the pinewood so that the blade cuts exactly through the outlines. Bend the pinewood when the blade begins to approach the flare part of the bell. As a beginner, you might not cut through the lines perfectly, but then, it is all about practice.
12. When you are done, turn of the scroll saw machine and pull out the pinewood plaque. You will notice that the bell shape comes out of the major piece.
13. Dab an adhesive remover on the outline sheet, wait for a few minutes, and then, peel it off.
14. You are done!

Cross

Now, this design will help you to practice how to cut through sharp points.

Materials

- A scroll saw device.
- ¾ inches pinewood of 3" by 4".
- Temporary bond spray adhesive or glue stick.
- Grade 5 skip-tooth blade.
- Drill with a ⅛" diameter bit.
- Adhesive remover or mineral spirit.

Procedures

1. With the drill, bore a blade entry hole through your pinewood at the uppermost sides.

2. Insert the grade 5 skip-tooth blade through the bored hole and then clamp it down with the upper grip.

   P.S: Before you clamp down the blade, ensure that the teeth point downward. You should also adjust the tension in the blade if necessary. Lastly, the blade must be at an angle of 90° to the table.

3. Make a clear photocopy of the outline of a cross design.

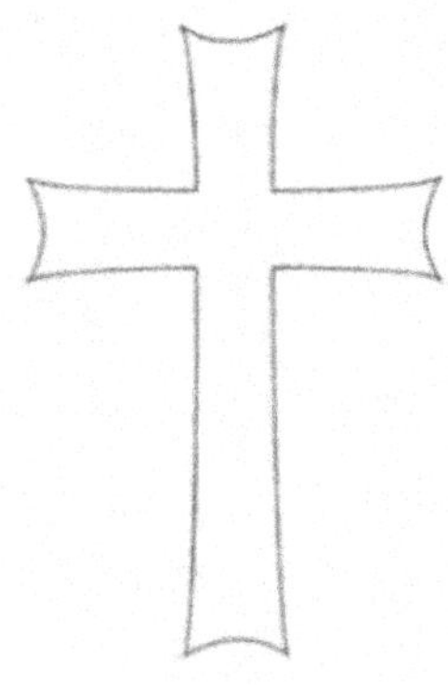

4. Spray the temporary spray adhesive behind the design outline and then wait for some moments for it to get sticky.
5. Press the outline on the surface of the pinewood while making sure that the length of the outline is lesser than the length of the side of the pinewood.
6. Turn on the scroll saw device and wait for the blades to begin to run at its normal speed.
7. Gently guide the hole you bored into the pinewood to the moving blade and then guide it through the outline of the cross.
8. When you want to cut through the wood, make sure you cut through the short four arcs first. After that, you can then proceed to cut the other eight longer lines. This will help you ensure that the arcs aren't cut as round bends but sharp edges.
9. When you are done cutting through the outline, turn off the scroll saw. Before you can free the plaque, unclamp the blade from its grip.
10. You'd notice that the cut-out cross design drops out from the major piece.
11. Dab a towel in an adhesive remover or mineral spirit.

12. Wait for some time for the glue to be weakened before pulling off the sheet of paper.

13. You are done!

Macaw Puzzle

This project combines the effects of curves and sharp edges so you can easily practice them.

Materials

- ⅝″ by 8″ by 17″ pinewood for the body
- ½″ by 2½″ by 8″ pinewood for the support.
- Temporary bond spray adhesive.
- Sandpaper of fine grits like the 220-grit adhesive.
- Small eyebolt.
- Wood stains or paint of the color you desire.
- Grade 5 skip tooth blade.
- Adhesive remover.

Procedure

1. Cut the pinewood into two—one for the major design and the other as the support. Meanwhile, you need to ensure that you cut several small plaques out of the major wooden plaque. For

puzzle designs, you will have to cut each puzzle piece separately. You cannot stack-cut.

2. Spray the back of the outline with the temporary bond spray adhesive. Do not spray the surface of the wood if you don't want to have issues getting the paper outline off after you are done cutting. Wait for a couple of seconds for the spray to get sticky.

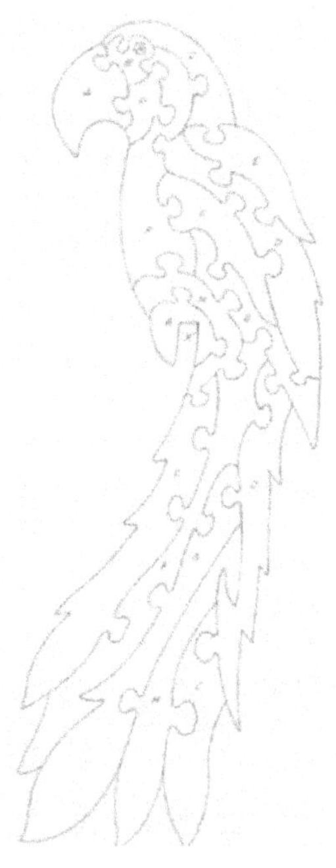

3. Attach the photocopied outline of the design to the major wood plaque and then press your palm across the surface to get rid of air bubbles.

4. Turn on the scroll saw device and wait for the blade to run at its normal effective speed.

5. Start at the exterior to cut through the outlines of the parrot first. Here, use the grade 5 blade. Next, move on to the interior pieces of the puzzle. Cut out the puzzle designs on the small wooden plaques' several pieces by repeating the above steps. Remember that each puzzle will have its own pattern so that interlocking will be possible.

6. When you are done, use the 220-grit sandpaper to sand each of the puzzle pieces. Make sure you follow the direction of the wood's graining to ensure that there are no incidents of chipped woods.

7. The next thing you need to do is to cut out the outline for the whole design. To do this, you will have to follow the pattern you used to cut off the exterior puzzle pieces. Ensure that the pattern of the platform for the puzzle pieces has the same density as each puzzle piece.

8. When you are done cutting out the outline of the whole puzzle, use a lint free cloth to wipe off the dust.

9. Now, the next thing to do is apply finish to the project. You can either paint it or use wood stains. Wood stains were used here though. You can go for wood stains that are clear enough and can be easily blended to strike the needful harmony. An example of this kind of wood stain is Wood burst.

10. To add color to the puzzle pieces, dab a towel that has been previously dipped into color across the surfaces of the puzzle pieces. You could decide to use an artist's brush to apply the paint too if you wish.

11. Wipe off the excess of the color by lightly dragging a towel across the surface of the paint puzzle piece. Go along with the grain of the wood when using a towel.

12. Leave the painted pieces to dry for bout two days.

13. Fix the eyebolt to the support.

14. Now, arrange the puzzle pieces along the major puzzle piece after dotting the surface with glue.

15. You are done!

Animal Toys

Materials

- One piece of a ¾″ by 12″ by 6″ of Medium Density Fiber-board (MDF).
- Two pieces of a ¾″ by 4″ by 3″ wood for the back legs.
- 2 pieces of wood of ¼″ inches with diameter of 2″ length.
- Temporary bond spray adhesive.
- Adhesive remover.
- Pencil.
- Sandpaper of 100 grits.
- Nail.
- A pair of scissors.
- Reverse tooth blades of grade number 9.
- Drill with bits of diameter of ⅛″, ¼″ or ⅜″.
- Hammer.

Procedures

1. Make a photocopied outline of the design you want to use for the body. Make two copies of design for the two legs. It has to be one for the right leg and the other for the right leg.

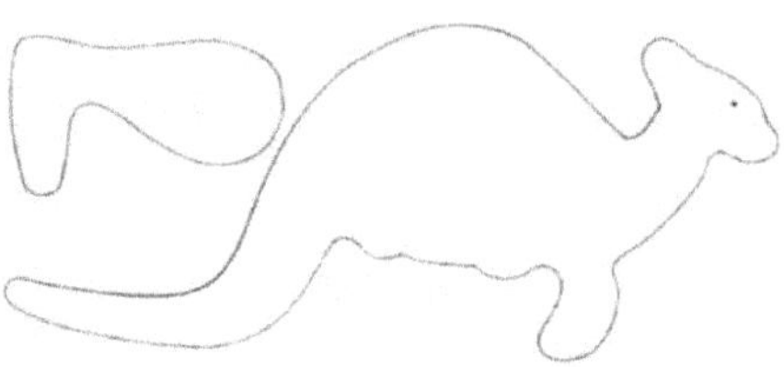

2. Cut the excess paper from around the design outline and make sure there is excess paper of about ⅛ inches left.
3. Now, move on to cutting the wood into the size you want to work on. Ensure the major wood has a size that is ¼ inches larger size than the size of the design outlines.
4. Spray the adhesive to the back of the three design outlines and wait for about thirty seconds for the sprayed adhesive to get sticky.
5. Fix the sticky outlines to the central surface of the wooden plaque. Place the outlines side by side on the same wooden plaque. This method will go a long way in managing the wood.

6. To cut out the two back legs, use a grade nine reverse tooth blade. Cut the main piece, too, with the same blade.

7. Drill two holes inside the two back legs with a ¼" diameter bit. Make sure that the holes are about ½" deep.

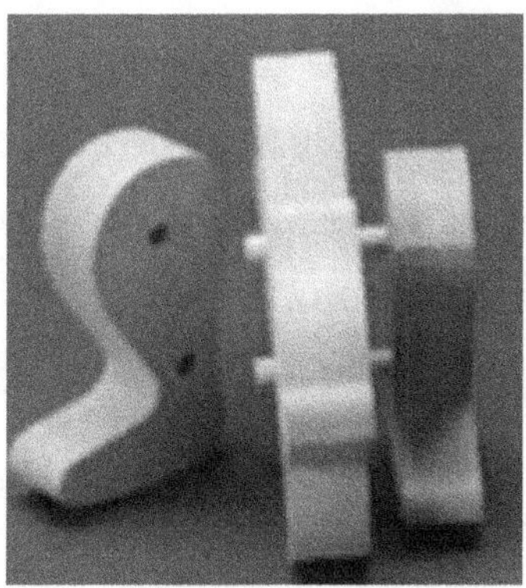

8. Use a ⅜" diameter bit to bore a hole through the belly of the main body.

9. Use a ⅛" diameter bit to bore holes for the eyes at either sides of the head.

10. Once you are done cutting and drilling holes into the design outlines, smoothen the surfaces with a sandpaper of 100-grits.

11. You can choose to paint the animal toy if you want. The animal wasn't painted here but you can either use wood stains or paint. If you would

like to blend the colors into each other, use wood stains.

12. The next thing to do is to join the toy's parts with pegs, nails or pins. Start with the hind legs first. Hammer the nails through the holes you previously drilled.

13. The next thing to do is to fix the main body to the two hind legs. Please make sure the dowels at the bottom of the legs fit into the body to allow for them to swing easily.

14. You may have to cut off a little wood from the bottom of the belly so that the legs can move freely. Leave about ⅛″ space between the major body and the legs.

15. You are done!

Wooden Gizmo Gears

This project is one that will help you to start making very accurate cuts. You would require the following materials along with a well of patience.

Materials.

- ¼″ by 16″ by 16″ of Baltic Birch plywood.
- ⅛″ by 1″ by 1″ of Baltic Birch plywood.

- Temporary bond spray adhesive.
- ¼" dowel, each 5" long.
- 100 grit sandpaper.
- Wood glue.
- Any wood finish of your choice.
- A grade 2 reverse-tooth blade.
- Drills with ¾" diameter drill bit.

Procedures

1. Cut the ¼ inch dowel into any suitable length.
2. Now, it is time to cut through the Baltic birch wood plaques. For designs that require several of the same pieces, you can use the stack cutting procedure. You can pile two layers of plywood on top of each other so that you can cut through them at the same time. Stack cutting will also help you see that the holes you drill occur at the same distance away from the wood frames.
3. Spray the temporary bond spray adhesive to the back of the wood. Wait for about thirty seconds for the spray to become sticky before going further to attach the outline to the wooden plaque's surface.

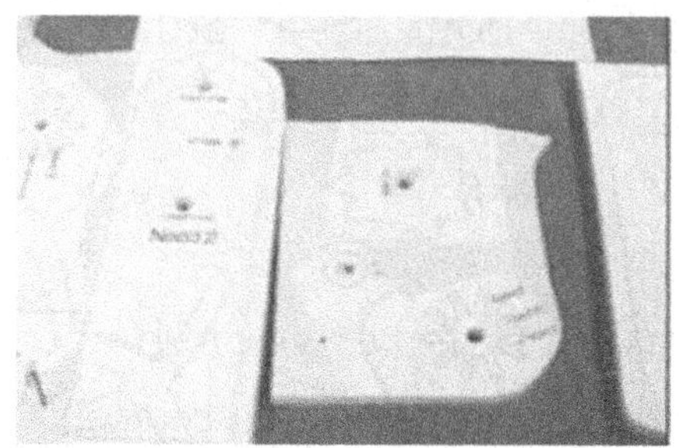

4. To cut out the gears, you can work with a reverse blade of grade 2. The essential parts of a gear that you should focus on cutting are the teeth's tips and edges. To get smooth cuts, start out from the base of the tooth.

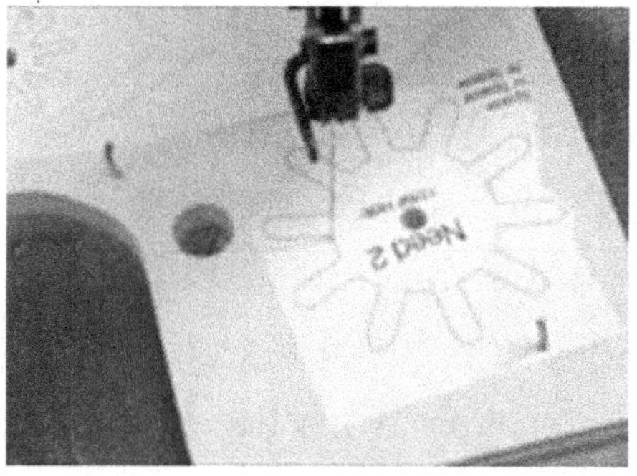

5. Smoothen the cut pieces using a 180- grit sandpaper. If you want to apply wood stain on the gears, do it now before assembling the parts.

6. Glue a ¼ inch spacer with a ¼ inch hole. Attach a ¼ inch thick dowel with a ¼ inch hole on the end of the ¾ inch piece.

7. Glue the dowel gear assembly into the ¼″ hole in the front of the design.

8. Fix all of the upright pieces to the base with glue. All the holes you made must tally with one another. To make sure of this, you can fix the dowels into the holes and roll them around to see that they spin freely. You should also ensure that the uprights sit squarely to the frame, no matter the directions.

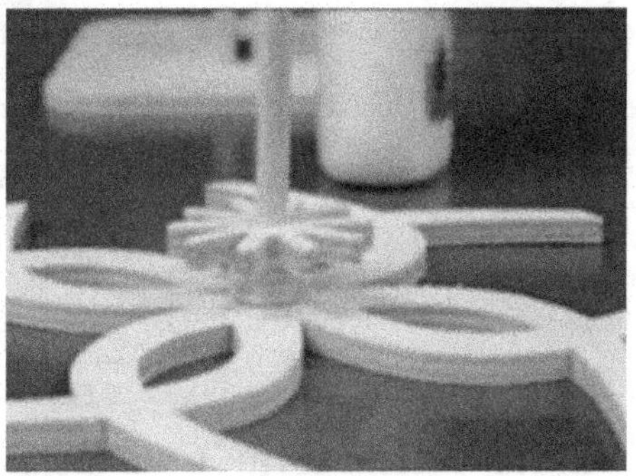

9. As you continue to put the pieces up, lay the spinner with the 17/64 inch hole on the table. Then, glue the ¼″ spacers and ⅛″ spacers to the 17/64 holes.

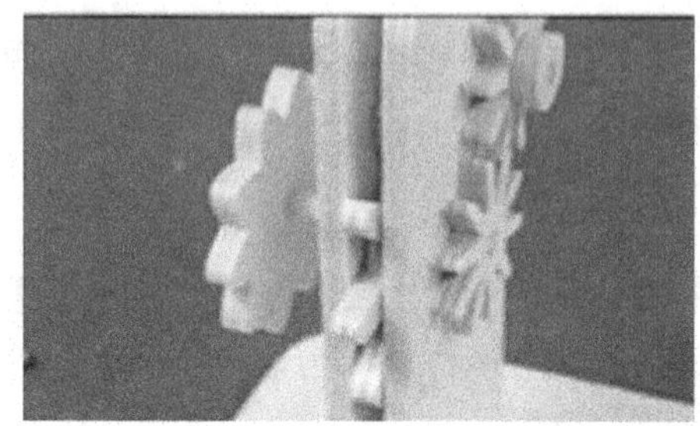

10. A dowel scrap can be fixed through the holes to align all the components. The assembly of parts needs to roll freely on the dowel.
11. Glue the wheel of the handle on the end of the 2⅛″ piece and ¼″ long dowel. Fix the dowel through the back of the upright frame.
12. Attach one of the large gears unto the dowel in between the two upright stands with glue.
13. Glue one of the small gears with the ¼ inch hole onto the end of the dowel. Make sure you leave enough space between the gears and the stands so that the whole fix moves freely.
14. Attach the other long gear with glue. That one will go between the two stands to the 2⅛″ long dowel when fixed firmly with the rear upright's back. At every point, as you go on, ensure that the dowel rolls freely.

15. Place the dowel gear assembly you made earlier (step 6) into the major shaft. Check if it still rotates freely.

16. Fix a ⅛″ spacer along with a 17/64 inch hole into the assembly's shaft.

17. Finish the assembly by finally attaching the spinner to the ¼ inch hole to the tip of the top shaft.

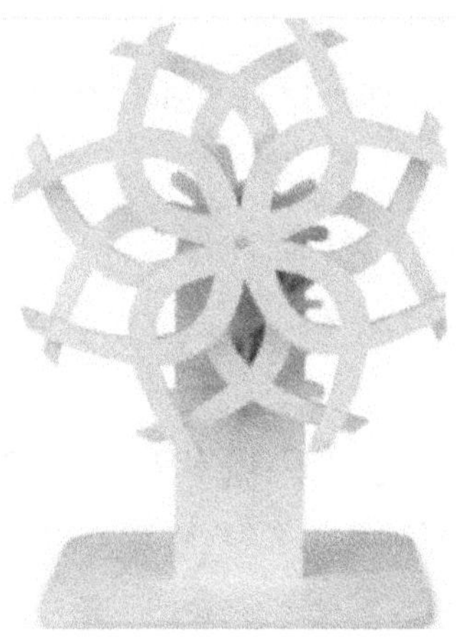

Inlay Earrings

Making inlay earrings will help you use up the scraps of hardwood left from your other scroll saw projects. It will also help you to see how creative you are.

Materials

- ¼ inch by 3 inch by 3 inch hardwood. Make sure they have different colors.
- Hot melted glue gun and glue sticks.
- Temporary bond spray adhesive or glue sticks.
- White glue.
- Sandpaper of 120-grits.
- Tung oil.
- Lint-free cloth.
- 6mm jump ring. You will need two of this ring.
- 4mm jump ring. You will also need two of this ring.
- Grade 3 regular-tooth blades
- Drills with a diameter of 1/16 inches diameter.
- Grade 63 drill bits.
- Needle-nose pliers.

Procedures

1. Make the photocopy of the pattern for your inlay earrings.

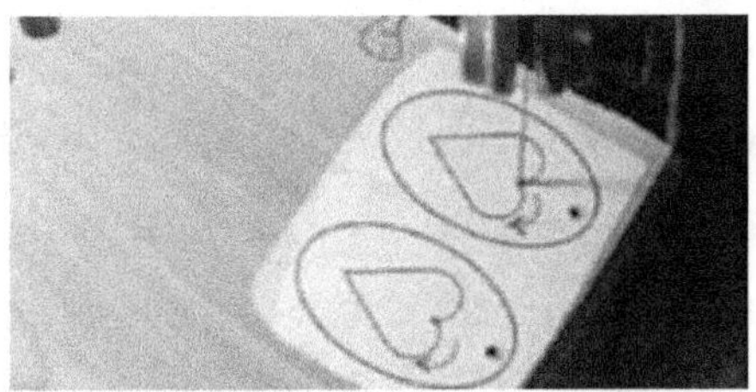

2. Spray the back of the outline with the temporary bond spray adhesive. Wait for a couple of minutes for it to get sticky.
3. Fix the pattern to the work piece's surface and then bore blade entry holes for the inlay sections with a grade 63 drill bit.

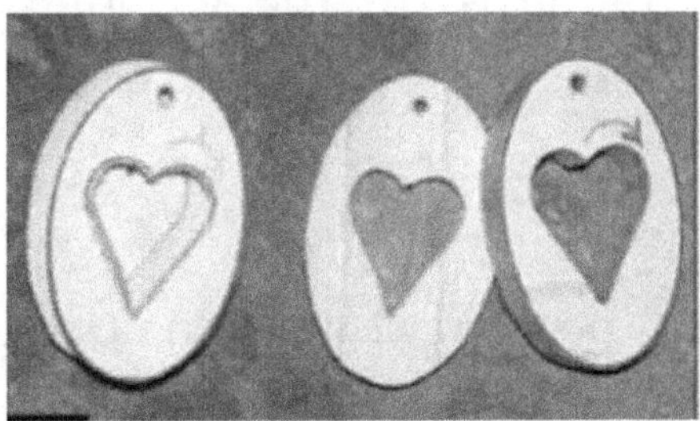

4. Bore the holes for the earring hooks with a 1/16 inch diameter bit.
5. Tilt your saw table to an angle below its usual horizontal plane.

6. Turn on your scroll saw device and then start cutting the moment the blade starts rolling at its effective speed.

7. In a case you start cutting out of the outline, you can slowly return to the original outline.

8. When you get to the bottom of the heart, hold the wood with your index finger and then gently pull the wood towards the back of the blade while simultaneously turning the wood around.

9. Cut the outlines of the earring. To do this, adjust the table so that it's square again. This way, you will have one set of inlay earrings and another set of silhouette heart earrings.

10. Peel the patterns off the wooden surfaces with adhesive removers.

11. Put the layers aside.

12. To see that the earrings have a perfect oval shape, smoothen the surface with an abrasive.

13. Insert the inlay into the earring using the white glue. Apply the glue in drops to any hole or line that isn't leveled with the outer panes of the earring.

14. Sand both sides of the earring while the glue hasn't yet dried to reduce its thickness to 1/16 inches.
15. Wait for the glue to dry.
16. Immerse each earring inside Tung oil to finish it.
17. Allow the oil set into place before using a lint-free cloth to wipe the excess off the surface.
18. Allow the earrings to dry.
19. The next thing you need to do is to fix the hooks inside the earring. To do this, twist open the 6mm jump ring using needle-nose pliers. Then, string it through the hole in the earring.

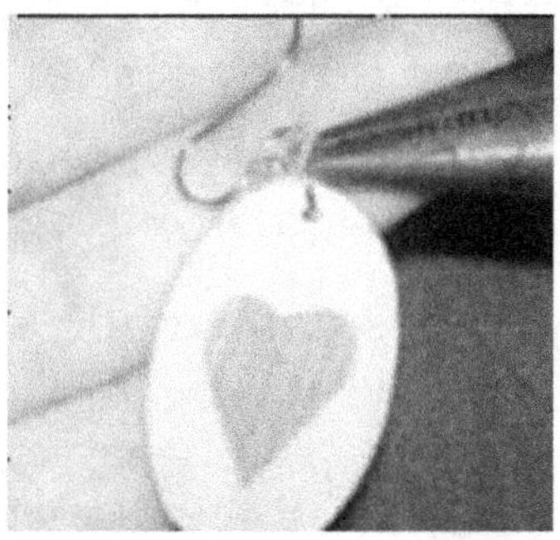

20. Close the jump ring.
21. Now, twist open the 4mm jump ring and then, string the 4mm ring through the 6mm ring.

22. After fixing the end of the hooked wire into the 4mm jump ring, close the 4mm ring.
23. You are done!

Salt and Pepper Shakers

For this project to come out nicely, you might need bits of expensive wood.

Materials

- ¼" by 2½" by 17" of Poplar wood.
- ¼" by 2½" by 4" of walnut wood.
- ¼" by 2½" by 4" of oak.
- 2 pieces of ¼" by 1½" by 1⅛" of walnut.
- ¼" by 1¼" by 1¼" of Poplar wood.
- 2 pieces of ¼" by 2" by 2½" scrap wood.
- ¼" by 2" by 2" of scrap wood.
- 4 pieces of ¼" by 2" by 2" of Poplar wood.
- Wood glue.
- Two each of ⅝" diameter corks.
- 4 pieces of ¾" by 1" by 3" scrap wood.
- Spray adhesive.
- Double-sided tape.
- Clear packaging tape.

- Different sandpaper grits.
- Clear finish of your choice.
- Grade 5 reverse-tooth blade.
- Drill with 3/32″ diameter bit.
- Belt sander.
- Awl.
- Pin.
- Toothpick.
- Two quick grip clamps.

Procedures

1. Cut out four designs for the pepper shaker patterns.
2. Spray the adhesives to one side of the outline and then wait for it to get sticky.
3. Fix the adhesive to the ¼″ by 2½″ by 17″ side of the shaker side. Now, cut through the design's outline.
4. Do not peel off the design yet. Place the salt and pepper shaker sides apart and let the patterns face down, away from your view.
5. Cut out right ½″ of the walnut and oak trim pieces and fix them to the sides of the shaker using the double-sided tape. Ensure that both of

the shakers have two sides with walnut and two sides with oak. Keep the trim pieces with the sides.

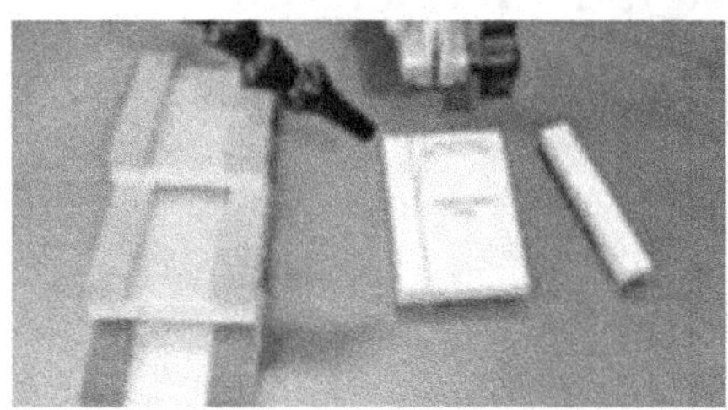

6. Set the trim pieces away from each other and fix the walnut and oak to the poplar sides. Keep the pieces in order so that they can fit in more closely.
7. Use a grip clamp to hold the trim pieces to the sides.
8. Wipe off any excess glue and make sure the sides are clamped for about 30 minutes. Leave the gum to dry for at least ten hours before you remove the design outlines.
9. To inlay the P center, pile the walnut and poplar inlays with the poplar wood on top.
10. With the table of your scroll saw device tilted, cut along the outlines of the letter.
11. Separate the piece again and then use a pin to apply glue into the walnut kerf and circle.

12. Clamp the kerf closed and insert the center of the 'P.' Leave it to dry.

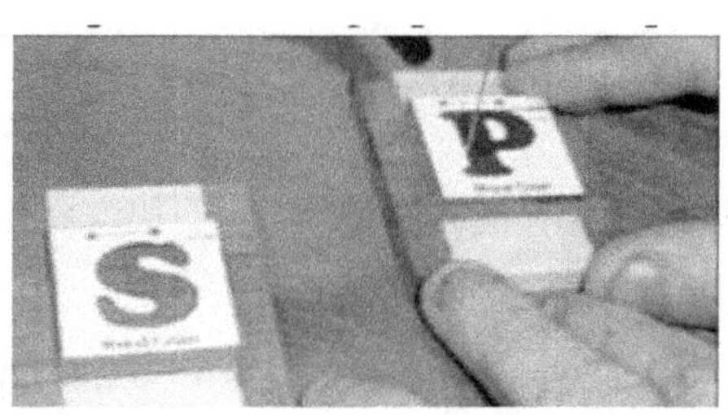

13. Attach the letter patterns using a pin to line up the P with the inner circle inlay.
14. On the two sides of the walnut trim, draw up a ⅝" line from the bottom. Line up the bottom of the inlay stock with lines and then fasten them together with a double-sided tape.
15. Tilt your table and cut through those lines again.
16. Assemble and sand the pieces. While the kerfs have been glued together and closed, glue in the inlays and let the glue dry.

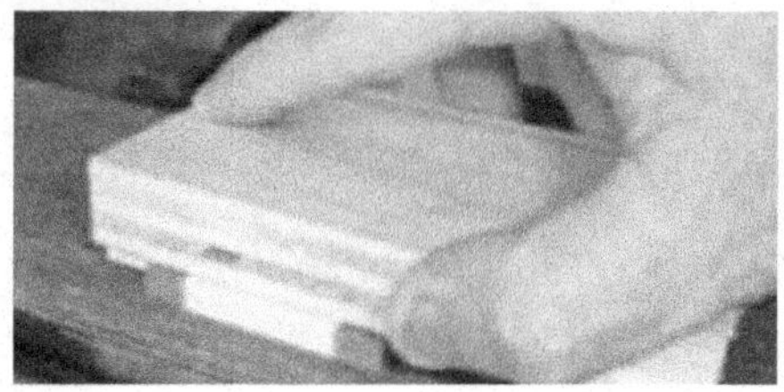

17. To make a holding jig, glue the ⅛" thick piece to the end of the larger piece of scrap wood. The ⅛" piece is to prevent the large piece from sliding off the table. Now, with the holding jig and belt sander, sand all the surfaces to make them smooth.

18. Now, it's time to make the box joint cuts. To do this, practice first on scrap wood so that you won't make errors while cutting the sides of the shaker. Lay one of the sides on a flat surface and keep the other side up, closely pressed to the flat surface. Mark the depths of the box with a pencil. Do this for all of the sides.

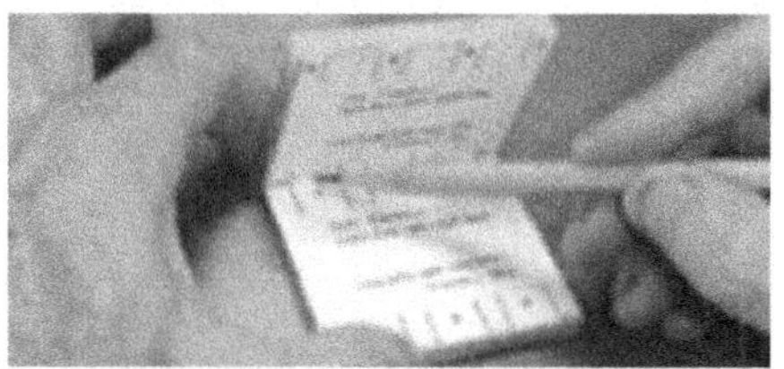

19. Now, square your blade to the table.
20. Cut right through the depth lines.
21. To finally assemble all the cuttings, fix the tail and pin outlines to the sides. Mark the depth lines

and cut the joints of the box. Spread glue onto the joints of the box and fix the sides together.

22. Clamp the shakers together.

23. After about ten minutes, wipe off any glue that may have snuck out of the joints before leaving it to dry for another ten hours.

24. Cut a hole in a scrap wood that matches with your cork. It should protrude with a length that is less than ¼". Fix the patterns to the bottom of the shakers, drill blade entry holes and then, cut circles that match your cork.

25. Drill holes and cut the stands and tops.

26. Level the surface of the top and bottom of the sides.

27. Glue and clamp the top and bottoms of the shakers and allow them to dry.

28. To finish the shakers, attach clear tape over the cork to prevent saw dust from getting in.

29. Sand the sides and corners with a belt sander and fix the shakers to their bottoms with glue.

30. Rub any finish of your choice on the surface of the wood.

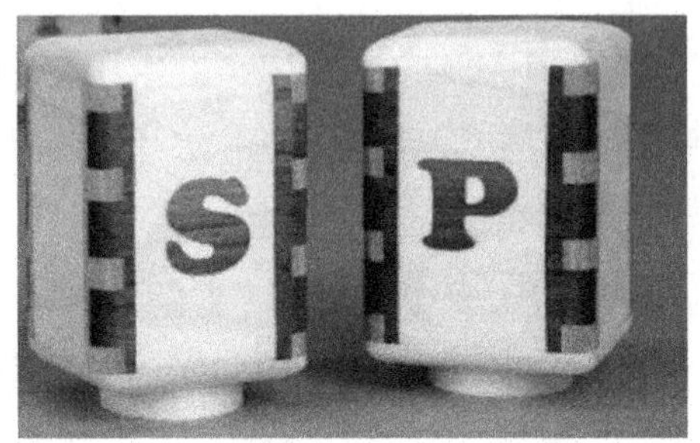

Desk Plaque Puzzles

Materials

- 1½ oak or maple with a length long enough to take the selected name.
- Temporary spray bond adhesive.
- Sandpaper (80 or 100 grits, 150, 220 grits).
- Mineral spirits.
- Gloss spray lacquer.
- Fine point permanent marking pen.
- Awl.
- Drill with ¹/16" hex shank bit
- Grade 2, Grade 0 and Grade 2/0 spiral blades.
- Grade 7 reverse-tooth blades.
- Razor blade.

- Router with ¼″ round-over bit.

Procedures

1. Make a photocopied outline of the design.
2. Spray the adhesive to the back of the outline and wait for it to get sticky.
3. Attach the outline to the center of the surface of the wooden plaque.
4. Turn on your scroll saw device and begin to cut through the outlines. When rounding over the edges of the design, use a ¼″ bit.
5. Now, when you are done, attach the second piece of wood to the first. Now that you have a woodblock that is 1½″ thick, sand the ends, bottom and top with a jointer, planer, or any other sanding tool.
6. Remove the design outlines with mineral spirits.
7. You can finish your project by spraying the surface with gloss spray lacquer.
8. You are done!

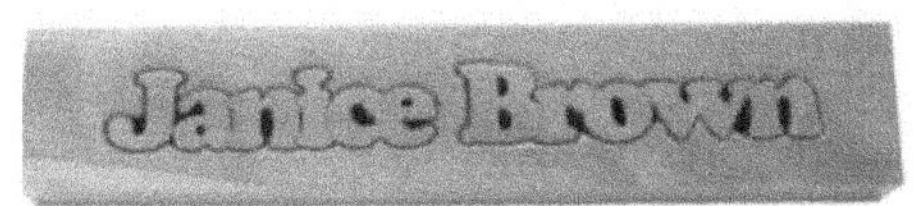

Mini Desk Clock with an Eagle

Materials

- ¼″ by 2½″ by 3″ of any hardwood for the eagle insert.
- ⅜″ by 1″ by 3½″ of any hardwood for the top and bottom.
- ¾″ by 3″ by 5″ of any hardwood for the clock body.
- 1⅜″ of wood for the clock insert.
- Wood glue.
- Oil finish.
- Spray varnishes.
- Reverse tooth blades of grade number three.
- Grade 7 or 9 reverse-tooth blades.
- Clamps.
- Sandpaper of 100, 150, 180, and 220 grits.
- 1⅜″ Forstner bit.
- Router.

Procedure

1. Start to sand the pieces with a 100-grit sandpaper.

2. Continue to sand the wood until you reach the 220-grit sandpaper.

3. Spray the back of your designs with a temporary bond spray adhesive. Wait for the spray to become sticky before you fix them to the wooden plaque.

4. Drill a blade entry hole for the interior cuts you will make. To get accurate and square holes, you can use a drill press.

5. To start cutting, use a grade 3 blade and run it through the inner outlines first.

6. From the inner outlines, work your blade out of the center.

7. Cut through the veins of the eagle's feathers carefully as well as the outline of the eagle's body. Use the grade 3 blade to cut through these lines before backing the blade out.

8. To cut the outer profile, use the grade 7 blade.

9. For the clock insert, drill a 1⅜" hole. Use the Forstner bit here. You could also cut the hole for the clock insert with the scroll saw. However, you may need to sand the insides a bit before the clock insert can fit in well.

10. Cut out the frame, top and base of the clock. Make these cuts by fixing a grade 7 blade to your scroll saw. Straighten the edges with a sandpaper.
11. Cut out the hole to the fretwork under the frame. Drill blade entry holes can be made near aside and cut out with a large blade. When you are done, round the edges with a router and a ¼″ diameter round over bit.
12. Round the edges of the top, frame and base of the clock using the router bits.
13. For the eagle insert, cut the ¼″ wide by ¼″ deep rabbet.
14. Run the sandpaper across the pieces lightly again. Any burr left behind by the saw blades should be removed by the 220-grit sandpaper.
15. Assemble the clock by using glue and a clamp to hold the frame together. Allow the glue to dry.
16. Flue the eagle insert to the frame, clamp down on it and then, leave it to dry overnight.
17. Finish your work with any oil finish of your choice. You could use polyurethane or spar lacquer.
18. Spray the finished work with a spray varnish.

19. Add the clock insert and fix it in the clock while following the manufacturer's instructions.
20. You are done.

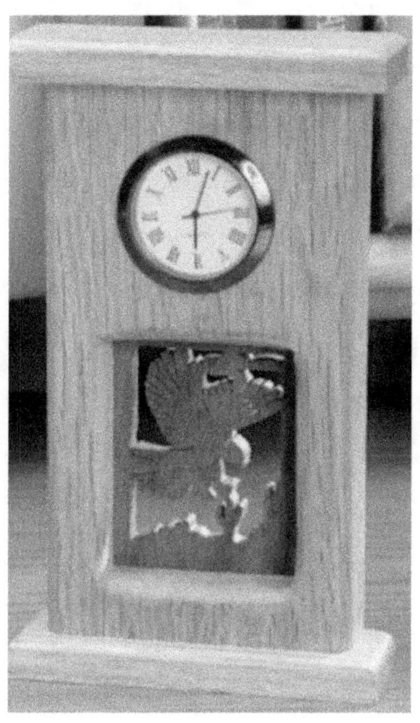

Music Box with Clock

Materials

- 1 piece of ½" by 4½" by 3" of walnut wood for the lid
- 1 piece of ⅛" by 4½" by 3" of walnut wood for the top lid.
- 11 pieces of ¼" by 4½" by 3½" wood for the base
- ⅛" dowels of lengths 3", 3", 2⅜"and ¾."
- Temporary bond spray adhesive.
- 200-grit sandpaper.
- Hinges.
- Yellow woodworker's glue.
- Epoxy glue.
- Music movement.
- Clock.
- ⅛" by 3½" by 2½" of thin plastic.
- 2½" felt pads.
- Finish of your choice.
- Drill of bit sizes ⅛", 3/16", 5/32".
- The grade 2 blade.
- Forstener bit of 1⅜" diameter for clock insert.

Procedures

1. Cut your wood so that there's still a space of ¼" at each corner. Then, sand the two and the bottom.

2. Photocopy the patterns you want to use.
3. Spray the back of the outline with the temporary bond adhesive. Wait for it to get sticky before fixing it to the wooden surface.
4. Drill out holes of ⅛″ in the walnut wood.
5. Now, you can start to cut out the pieces. To do this, work with a grade 2 blade.
6. After, you can sand lightly.
7. Drill the 3/32″ and ⅛″ holes in the third weave. The hole must be big enough to accommodate the dowel's free movements.
8. You can glue the parts next. Use two of the 3″ by ⅛″ dowels as a guide for the main time. Start gluing from weave 1. Lie the first weave to the second weave, the second weave to the third weave, and so on. Make sure that the glue does not get to the ⅛″ dowel at the right side.
9. After the glue has set, remove the dowel from the right side.
10. With a drill press, drill a 5/32″ diameter hole on weave 7.
11. Glue the dowel. If you feel it's important, you can drill the ⅛″ dowel in place too.

12. Glue the other dowel. Glue a ⅜" long and ⅛" dowel in place at the right side at the bottom.

13. Drill the ³/32" diameter hole through the ⅛" diameter hole in the right side. Drill into weave number 12 and weave number 7.

14. Make the plastic window by drilling ³/32" holes in it. Cut out this material with the pattern you have in hand.

15. Cut the ring for the spacer before you can add the clock insert.

16. Make a hole for the insert using a Forstener bit of 1⅜" diameter. The hole has to be ⅛" deep. Go slowly here so that the wood doesn't cave in as you push the drill in.

17. Glue the spacer ring using the woodworker's glue. Then, make sure the clock insert fits in properly.

18. Fix the top lid and lid to the hinge. Make sure they fit snugly together.

19. Rout the lid.

20. Glue the hinge to the top lid and lid using epoxy.

21. Screw the music movement in place. To suit it, cut and bend the on or off wires. See to it that the on or off wire moves about freely.

22. Use two small screws to add the plastic window.
23. Add an on or off dowel that is ⅛". To suit its purpose, make sure it is 2⅛" long. See to it that this dowel also moves up and down and turns the music movement on and off when the lid opens. To help hold the on or off wire in place, notch the bottom end of the dowel.
24. If necessary, file the insides of the metal hinge so that the on/off dowel moves up and down freely.
25. Finish the project however you like. You could use polyurethane aerosols or Tung oils. Tung oils will not seal the pores of the wood. Instead, their lightness allows the wood to actually breathe. You'd even get a finer finish with a shiny look.
26. Add felt pads to the bottom of the project.
27. You are done!

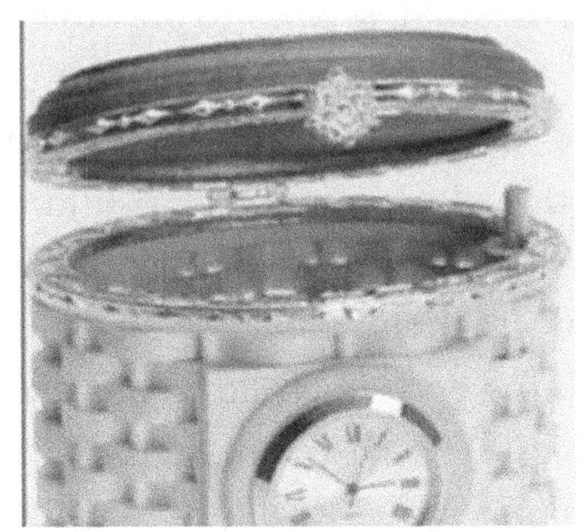

Monogram Keepsake Box

Materials

- ⅛" by 6" by 6" of MDF.
- 2" by 6" by 6" of any hardwood of your choice for the main box.
- 5/16" by 6" by 6" hardwood of your choice for the backer board
- Temporary bond spray adhesive.
- Different grits of sandpaper up to 400 grits.
- Wood glue of choice.
- PVA glue of choice.

- Flocking color.
- Poster paint that tallies with the color you use for flocking.
- Finish of your choice.
- Grade 12 skip-tooth scroll saw blade.
- Belt sander, oscillating sander or disc sander. You don't have to have these though.
- Router with a ⅛" diameter round bit.
- Different kinds of clamp.
- Rotatory power carver.
- Small paintbrush.

Procedures

1. Get a photocopied outline of the pattern you want to use for the keepsake box. Spray the temporary bond spray adhesive at the back of the outline and wait for it to get sticky.
2. Fix the sticky outline to the 2" by 6" by 6" hardwood.
3. Use a grade 12 skip tooth blade to cut the outer profile. After cutting, make sure that the grain of the backing board is oriented with the grain of the major box body.

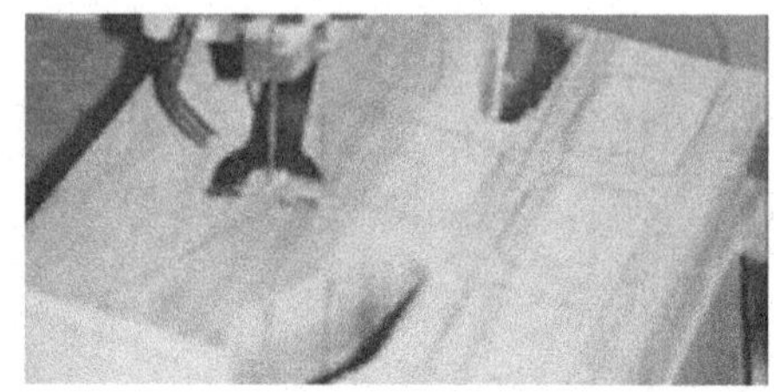

4. Using the same grade 12 blade you used above, cut the backer board.

5. Now, to cut out the drawers of the keepsake box, start at the bottom and cut up to the drawers at the top.

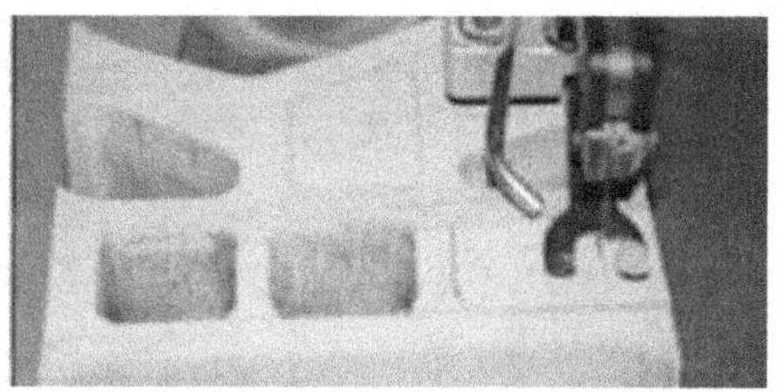

6. Turn the scroll saw device off and then, slide the blade to the next lower drawer. Power the saw again and begin to cut around the perimeters of the drawer.

7. Since the kerf of the blade is small and the scroll saw blades cut cleanly, you can easily glue the cuts later. To cut out the drawers, you could also drill small blade entry holes but then, small

diameter bits and small scroll saw blades used for interior outlines can easily break in this kind of thick wood.

8. Cut 7/16" from the front and ¼" from the back of each drawer. Mark and cut the center sections out of the drawer. Make sure that the walls of the drawers are at least, 1/50" thick.

9. Sand the ends of the cuts to ensure a tight fit. Apply thin layers of glue to the center of the drawer and then, position the front and back in place. Until the glue dries up, the front and back must be held in place by rubber bands.

10. Apply glue to the cuts at the bottom and then, work the glue into the joints with a knife.

11. Clamp the pieces together and make sure that you do not glue the saw cuts through the drawer compartments. You will later detail these compartments with a V-shaped cut later.

12. Use a belt sander to smoothen the flat surfaces and a vertical oscillating sander for the rounded sections. To remove the marks from the belt sander, use a 9" diameter disc sander with a soft rubber backing fitted with 220-grit sandpaper.

13. Finally, you can smoothen the piece with a 400-grit sandpaper.

14. Use a router with a ⅛" diameter round over bit to round off the edges of the box. You could also use a sandpaper if you prefer that. Make sure that you do not round off the bottom of the box. Round off the edges of the box with a sandpaper. To add V-shaped cuts to mark the lines between the drawers, use a rotary power carver and a cut off bit.

15. Cut out 3/14" thick straps from the scrap portion of the box backer. Cut out 5/8" long pieces from the strips and round the corners on one end. To do this, you could use a flip sander or sandpaper. Flatten the square end on a sander until the piece is ½" long. Now, glue these pulls to the front of the drawers.

16. Apply any finish of your choice to the keepsake box. You could use Tung oil, Danish oil or gloss lacquer.

17. You can decide to line the insides of the drawers with PVA glue. Paint the insides with the glue and leave it to dry for about ten minutes before adding another layer of the glue.

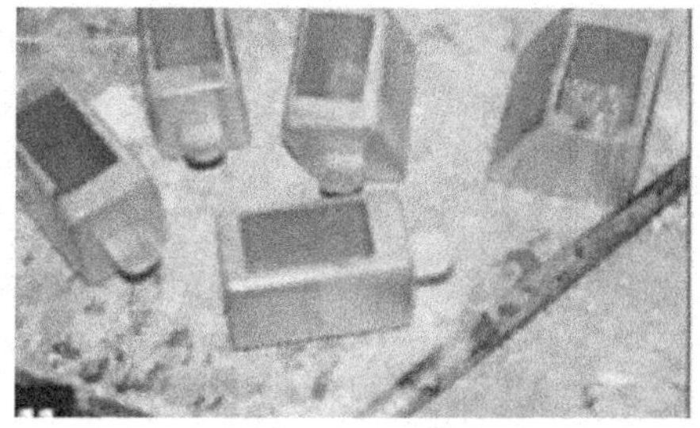

18. You are done!

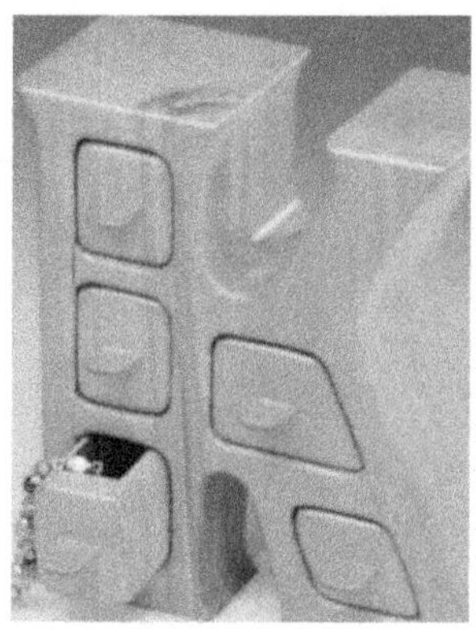

Woven Basket

Materials

- 3/16″ by 3¾″ by 5¾″ of aspen for the top.
- 2 pieces of 3/16″ by 3¾″ by 5¾″ of aspen for the base and lid.

- 1/8″ by 2¾″ by 4⅜″ of aspen wood for the lid liner.
- Three pieces of ⅜″ by 4¾″ by 5¾″ aspen.
- Two pieces of ⅛″ dowel, each 2¼″ long.
- 7/8″ by 1½″ by 3¼″ of black walnut for the handle.
- Flocking material.
- Temporary bond spray adhesive.
- Sandpaper of finer grit.
- Tack cloth.
- Woodworker's glue.
- Cellophane tape.
- Turpentine.
- Skip tooth blades of grade 2 and 5.
- Reverse tooth blades of grade 5.
- Drill with ⅛″ diameter bits.
- Clamps or rubber bands.
- Steel wool, #0000.

Procedure

1. Cut the aspen wood to the dimensions given above.
2. Sand the top and bottom surfaces lightly with a fine-grit sandpaper.

3. Wipe the saw dust off the surface with a lint-free cloth.

4. Make a photocopied outline of the pattern.

5. Spray the back of the pattern with a temporary bind spray adhesive. Wait for the glue to get sticky before applying it on the wooden surface.

6. Drill the line-up holes with a ⅛″ bit. Also, be careful when drilling the ⅛″ diameter line-up holes in each part. Do not drill holes into the lid.

7. Drill blade entry holes where they are needed using the same drills and bits that you used for procedure 6.

8. Cut out the top, lid, base and lid liner using a grade 5 reverse tooth blade.

9. Cut the interiors of the five portions using the grade 5 blade. You can make a line-up line saw kerf at the left side. This line is what you will follow to assemble the basket.

10. Cut out the center oval of the segment. Cut along the dashed line marked 'A'.

11. At the areas marked 'B' , cut straight in and back out. Be sure to make a total of 20 saw kerfs in each segment using the grade five skip-tooth blade.

12. Cut the scalloped edges with a grade 2 skip-tooth blade. There are several ways to get this kind of edge done. Place the work piece behind the table and then, slide the work piece into the back of the blade so that the back rests in saw kerf 'B'. While following the pattern line, cut the next Kerf which can either be to the right or left, all depending on how you want to move. Create one curved edge, then cut in a relatively straight line before creating the second curved edge. Repeat this steps 20 times, each time for each segment.

13. Cut and smoothen the dowels. On a flat surface, glue the two line up dowels to the base. Slide one segment over the dowels and then, glue it in place.

14. Finish gluing the segments. Take the next segment, turn it over and slide it unto the two dowels. Glue each segment in place with just a dab of glue. As you add each segment, make sure you alternate it up-and-down to have a woven effect.

15. Glue the top in place and then, smoothen the bottom so that the ends of the dowels are closely

joined to each other. Use clamps to hold the assembly of segments together until the glue sets.

16. Center and glue the lid liner to the lid. To know how to place the lid, follow the dashed lines on the base and the pattern of the lid for placement.

17. Make the cut for the compound handle. First thing to do is to fold the pattern of the handle along the dashed line and then, glue the pattern to the wood with a temporary spray adhesive.

18. Drill two blade entry holes with a ⅛″ bit. Then, make the two interior cuts of the loop using a grade 5 skip tooth blade.

19. Make the outer cuts along the top of the handle. Let your blade pass through the thicker of the two sides.

20. Reassemble all the pieces and hold them with a cellophane tape.

21. Finish the handle and turn it through an angle of 90°.

22. Center the handle on the lid and glue it into place.

23. Dab the whole basket with the #0000 steel wool whole making sure to follow the grains of the

wood. To clear the dust off, you can use a lint-free cloth.

24. You can choose to add stains to your project if you please.

25. For a finer interior, you can line the insides with flocking.

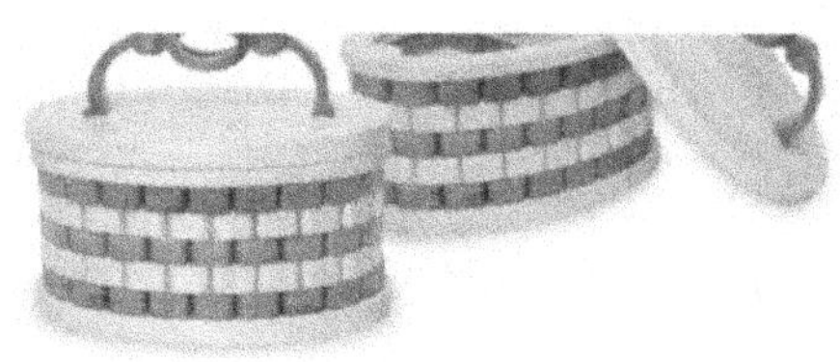

Classic Corner Shelf—Fretwork

Materials

- ¼" by 4½" by 16" wood choice for thin side piece.
- ¼" by 4¾" by 16" for wide side piece.
- ¼" by 4" by 4" for top shelf.
- Two pieces of ¼" by 5" by 5" for the middle and bottom shelves.
- Small brads.

- Double-sided tape.
- Different kinds of sandpaper.
- Wood glue.
- Adhesive.
- Clear spray finish.

Procedure

1. Cut the wood you chose to work with using the dimensions given above.
2. Sand the pieces with all the grits you have, starting from the roughest to the finest. You can end at 220-grits.
3. Stack the two side and lower shelves and use the double sided tape to hold them together.
4. Fix the pattern of your design to the surface of the wood at the top of the stack. Use a 1/16″ bit for the interior cuts. For the veining details, use the smallest diameter drill bit that you know a grade 2 blade will fit through.
5. Drill a 1/64″ diameter hole to join the sides and the shelves.
6. Cut the veining details; cut with a grade 2/0 reverse tooth blade. For interior cuts, use grade 1 reverse-tooth blades.

7. Cut out the perimeter of the sides using a grade 3 reverse tooth blade.

8. Assemble the shelves by applying a dot of glue along the end grain of the thinner side piece. Line up the piece and hold it in place while you drive the small brads in place.

9. Leave the glue to dry overnight before applying glue to the square ends of the shelf. Line then up after that and then, nail them in place.

10. Apply a clear spray finish of your choice.

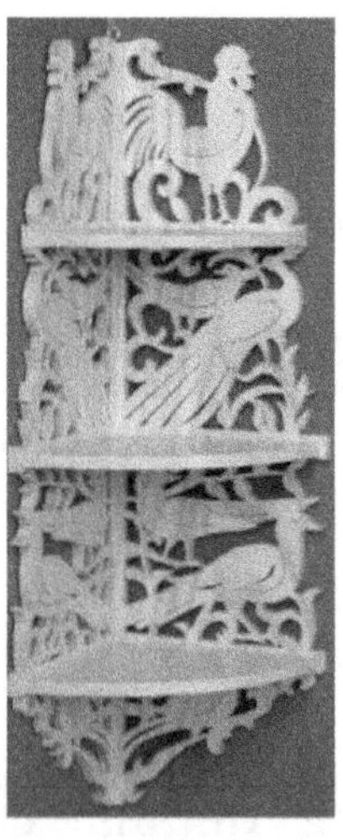

Compound Birds

This is a very easy and quick project

Materials

- 3/4" by 1½" by 4½" of pine wood.
- Use any finish of your choice.
- Spray adhesive.
- Clear tape.
- Thin scrap to hold the pieces together.
- Scroll saw blades with 12.5 teeth-per-inch.

Procedure

1. Photocopy the outline of the design for the two birds
2. Fold the design into two, where each half contains each bird
3. Cut out one and then, spray the adhesive to the back of the outline. Attach it to the pinewood.
4. Cut out each of the patterns with a scrap wood below it to hold in place the piece that gets cut out eventually.

5. After cutting, remove the outlines from the two cuttings with an adhesive remover.
6. Remove the scrap pieces of wood from the project until you are left with the actual design of the birds.
7. If you want, you can add wood stains to the cuttings. Any oil finish will do too.

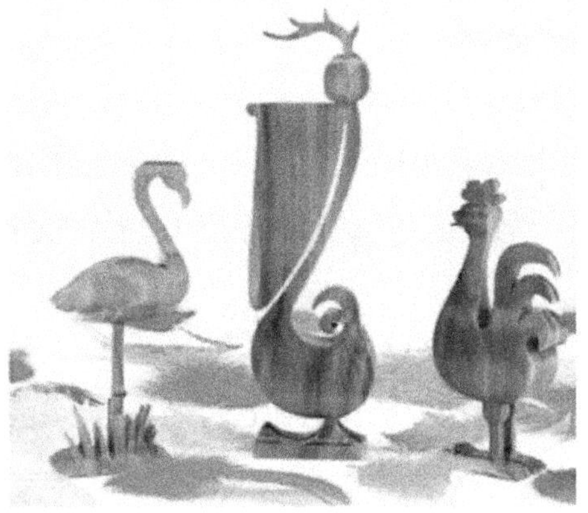

Decorative Foliage Votive Holder

Materials

- 3 pieces of 1⅜″ pieces of Maple wood for the leaf side pieces.

- 3 pieces of 1⅜" by 1⅝" by 3¼" wood.
- 1/2" by 3" by 3" wood.
- Spray adhesive.
- Clear packaging tape.
- Sandpaper of 220 grits.
- Spray lacquer.
- Votive cup.
- Cyanoacrylate glue.
- Grade 3 and 5 skip-tooth blades.
- Drill with 1/16" diameter drill bit.

Procedure

1. Attach the pattern after you must have sprayed the adhesive to the back surface of the Maple wood.
2. Cut out the veins on the patterns. Drill blade entry holes with a 1/16" diameter drill bit. Cut the leaf veins with a grade 3 skip-tooth blade. Do this step for all of the 6 leaves.
3. Drill a blade entry hole with a 1/16" diameter drill bit. Cut the inside of the design with the same blade.
4. Use a grade 5 skip tooth blade to cut out the outlines of the leaf. Set one wooden plaque on the

saw table so that the leaf's shape faces upwards. Don't remove the leaf from the block of wood after cutting the leaf's outline though. Keep the two pieces wrapped with clear packaging tape.

5. Cut out the profile of the leaves with a grade 5 skip tooth blade.

6. Free the cutting from the plaque after removing the tape carefully from the sides.

7. Sand all the pieces with a 220-grit sandpaper to remove the rough edges.

8. Glue the project together while making sure to avoid clamping the irregularly shaped pieces. Use the cyanoacrylate glue to attach the leaf pieces to the 'C' part.

9. Finish the candle holder. Apply a coat of Danish oil and several coats of spray lacquers.

10. You can now place the votive cup in position.

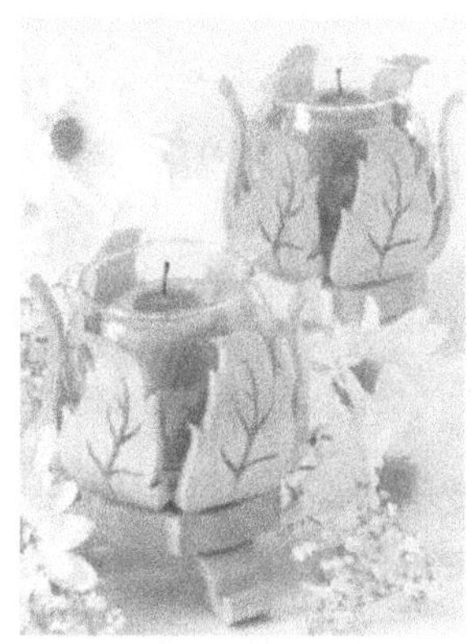

Lighthouse Silhouette

Materials

- ½" – ¼" by 8½" by 10½ inches.
- Sandpaper of 120, 180, and 220 grits.
- Temporary bond spray adhesive.
- Any oil finish of your choice.
- Saw tooth hanger.
- ½" blade for hardwood.
- Grade 5 reverse-tooth blade.
- Drill press with a small diameter drill bit.

Procedure

1. Smoothen the surface of your wooden plaque with a 120-grit sandpaper.
2. Wipe the sawdust off with a lint-free cloth.
3. Proceed to using the 180-grit sandpaper. If you do not clean off the dust after you sanded with the 120-grit sandpaper, you could risk scratching the wood. Wipe off the wood again and apply the pattern to it using a temporary bond spray adhesive.
4. Drill all blade entry holes.
5. Cut out the pieces. Start out on the inside with the more delicate interior cuts and then, work your way out.
6. Give the piece a final sanding with the 220-grit sandpaper
7. You can use an oil finish to finish your work. This oil will give it a satin smooth look. Hang your project as desired with a saw-tooth hanger.

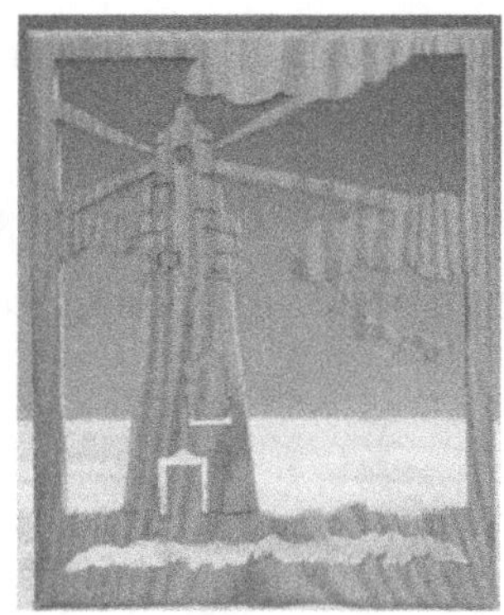

Celtic Anniversary Claddagh

Materials

- ½″ by 12″ by 9″ Walnut.
- Temporary bond spray adhesive.
- Woodworker's glue.
- Gloss clear wood finish.
- Sandpaper of 180 and 220 grit.
- Lint-free cloth.
- Table saw.
- Grade two blade.
- Drill with ⅛″ and 1/16″ diameter bits.

Procedures

1. Use a 180-grit sandpaper to smoothen the surface of the wood.
2. Use the lint-free cloth to wipe off the saw dust.
3. Get a photocopied outline of the design.

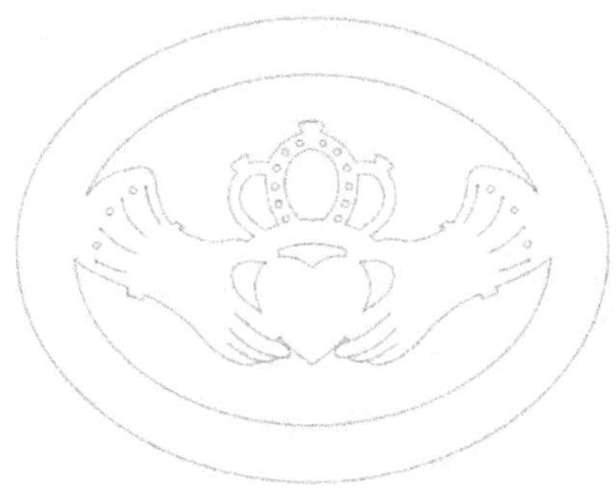

4. Spray the adhesive to the back of the outline and then, wait for it to get sticky.
5. Attach the outline of the Claddagh pattern to the wooden plaque.
6. Drill the blade entry holes into the glove and the crown. Use a ⅛″ bit. The holes for the glove at the ends of the line should be drilled with a 1/16″ bit. You could use a moto tool for drill in the holes because it is way better than having to shift the wood around the drill press.

7. Make the inside cuts. Cut the smaller areas first and leave the larger areas so that you can add supports to them. As you make these delicate cuts, be careful of the points where you lay your fingers because some of them can be easily broken under the pressure of your hands. Place your hands at the outer edges instead.

8. Cut out the letters, numbers and comma. Make sure you have a blade entry hole for each piece of the letters and numbers and one for the comma. You have to ensure that the letters and numbers look as identical as possible, so it would be great if you occasionally took breaks as you worked.

9. Cut the outside of the plaque after all the inside details have been completed.

10. Finish sanding the project with a 220-grit sandpaper. You don't need to sand the inside of the project because a well tensioned and positioned blade will make smooth cuts.

11. Wipe the surface of the wood to get rid of sawdust before applying any finish.

12. Two coats of gloss clear can be used to finish your projects. The aerosol spray is more preferable to the liquid one.

13. You are done!

Step Stool Name Puzzle

Materials

- Hammer.
- 1½″ of Maple wood.
- Temporary bond spray adhesive.
- Sandpaper of 80, 100 and 220 grits.
- Gloss spray lacquer.
- Awl.
- Drill with 1/14″ hex shank bit.
- Router with ¼″ round over bit.
- Reverse tooth blades of grade seven.
- Spiral blades of grade two.

Procedure

1. Make a photocopied outline of your pattern. Make sure the spacing between the letters is reduced considerable and that the letters overlap one another.

2. Drill the blade entry holes for the interior cuts. You can use a bit of any size. Next, drill a hole in the waste so you can cut out the first letter. The position of the drilled holes aren't important much. Just make sure they're not in places that will come out visibly in your finished work.
3. Use a grade 7 reverse tooth blade to make all of the inside cuts.
4. Cut out the first letter completely and remove it from the main piece. Then, cut out the other letters the same way.
5. Round the shapes using a ¼" round-over bit.
6. Cut the dovetails to attach the legs. If you don't want to use dovetails, you can drill in screw holes into your wood.
7. Assemble the stool.
8. Add a ⅛" backer. Fix thus backer beneath the stool so that the letters have a place to lie upon.
9. Apply your finish. You could either use Polyurethane or oil finishes.

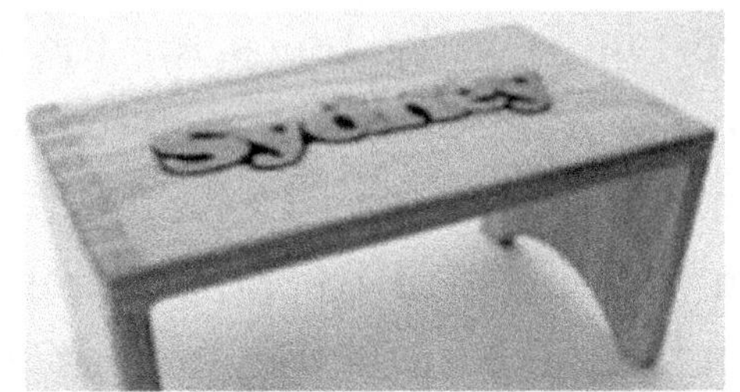

Sydney

Chapter 5

Fixing Common Scroll Saw Problems

Issues related to the heat generated by the scroll saw
Heat generally reduces the efficiency of a machine as some of its work will be wasted in this form. So, if this issue occurs with your scroll saw device, what could be the cause? If you overwork your device, it will overheat. Also, dull blades, wrong blade choices, and heavy thick materials can contribute to a scroll saw emitting a lot of heat.

Remedy: Make sure you use the right blade on the right wood. Big blades are meant for thick wooden plaques, and smaller blades for less dense plaques. Don't get confused. Unplug the machine from the socket and allow the machine to cool off for a while once you notice it's getting too hot. If the heat issue persists despite you doing all of the things above, make sure that you contact the saw manufacturer.

Exploded fuses and breakers
Fuses help to regulate the rate at which current flows into a circuit. In a scenario where the excess current

flows through the circuit, the wire in it melts and stops the current flow. If this happens to your scroll saw device, it may be because there is a flow of excess current through to the motor. This will immediately prevent your saw from working.

Remedy:

1. Check the fuse box immediately and change any of the melted wires you see there.
2. After doing this, plug your device into a source of stable electricity and reduce the blade's speed, and then, as you work, you could increase it some more.
3. Just see that you don't pass the speed limit of the saw.

Table vibrations

This can be a very serious issue if you are cutting with a parallel arm scroll saw. The components are usually prone to vibration, and it gets worse when you are cutting a thin plaque of wood.

Remedy: Ensure that you place your scroll saw on a leveled surface. If you are cutting with a prone to vibration device, it would be better if you used it to cut hardwood that has more resistance to it. However, if you have to work with a softwood, secure the plaque to the table by using a C clamp. Buying a bigger scroll saw that isn't prone to vibration could be another great way to fix this issue.

Blade tensions

Once your blade starts cutting with less accuracy and precision, you might need to increase or decrease your blade's tension immediately.

Remedy: Pluck the middle of the blade and listen to the sound it makes. A very sharp ping sound means that the blade is under a lot of tension. However, a weak sound could mean that it is under tension. To know how tensioned it is, you can compare the sound with another perfectly tuned blade and see how different the sound is. Adjust until you are satisfied.

Twisted blades

You would get a twisted blade when you start cutting through materials that you are not familiar with. In a case where the material is harder than you expected, it could cause your blade to get dented.

Remedy: Use the blade on the right plaque. In case the blade is already twisted, make sure that you change it.

Broken blades

This issue is a very common thing in scroll saws. Your blade will break if it is under too many tensional forces. If the blade breaks at the upper clamp, it may mean that it was clamped too tightly.

Remedy: Reduce the blade's tension and adjust the grip of the clamps until they grip the blade just firmly. If the blade has broken already, change it.

Reduced blade precision

Once your blade stops cutting through the lines of your patterns, it could be that it is under-tensioned or with a blunt tip. If the artist is not feeding the wood gently into the blade but is rather pressing it hard against it, the blade's precision would be greatly reduced.

Remedy: Increase the tension on the blade or change it. Do not force the wood on the blade. Your job is to guide it through the outline of your design. It will cut it.

Loss of steep cuts

This can happen if the blade is not square to the table surface or under the right amount of tension. Also, guiding your wood to the blade with so much force that the blade is pushed to the side can cause the cuts to lose their perpendicularity.

Remedy: Don't force the wood on the blade. Also, ensure that the blade is at right angles to the wood. You can also try increasing the tensional forces on the wood.

Uncontrollable blade
This issue arises mostly when cutting through thin wood. It could also be because the blade is moving too fast or that you are guiding it to the running blade at a very high speed.

Remedy: Decrease the speed of the blade. Feed the blade more slowly to the blade. When cutting through thin wood, you can try fixing a wood scrap to the bottom.

Excessive burning of wood when cutting
This is not Pyrography, where wood burning is the real deal. If you see burns in the wood when cutting through it, know that it is either because you are using the wrong blade size or type.

Remedy: Use a painter's tape to transfer your patterns. The glue usually moistens the blade as it cuts through the wood and eradicates the burning issue. When cutting hardwood, work with a large blade or one that is meant to cut through hardwood.

Excessively jumping workpiece
This issue could occur in a case where the undersides of the workpiece are not smooth and even. A wrongly inserted blade can also cause this issue.

Remedy: Before you start cutting, see to it that the teeth of the blade projects downwards. Run an abrasive across the underside of the workpiece to sit flat on the table of the saw.

<u>The end... almost!</u>

Hey! We've made it to the final chapter of this book, and I hope you've enjoyed it so far.

If you have not done so yet, I would be incredibly thankful if you could take just a minute to leave a quick review on Amazon

Reviews are not easy to come by, and as an independent author with a little marketing budget, I rely on you, my readers, to leave a short review on Amazon.

Even if it is just a sentence or two!

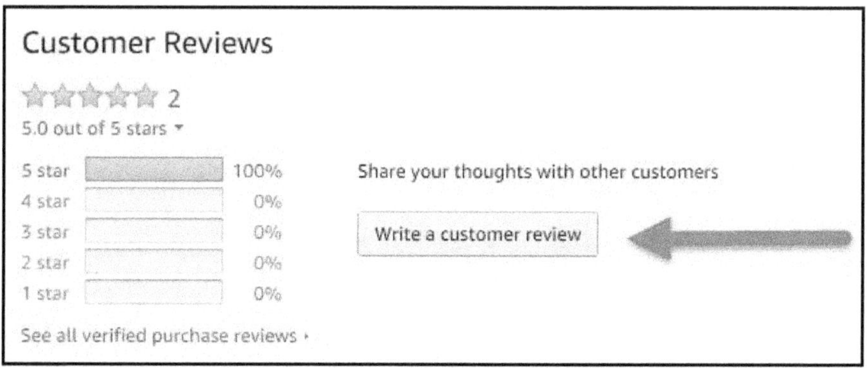

So if you really enjoyed this book, please...

>> Click here to leave a brief review on Amazon.

I truly appreciate your effort to leave your review, as it truly makes a huge difference.

Chapter 6

Scroll Saw Frequently Asked Questions

What kind of blade can cut in any direction?
Only spiral blades can cut in any direction. All you need to do is guide the project around the blade, and then, when it is time to change angles, you can turn the wood in that direction.

How long does it take to master the techniques of the scroll saw?
The answer to this isn't fixed. The time for learning varies from person to person. It also depends heavily on how much time and patience a person is willing to devote to learning the art. The more a person practices, the better he or she becomes.

How can the speed of my saw be reduced?
This issue depends on the kind of saw you are working with. Some saws have a variable speed button, while the other ones do not have one. Getting a scroll saw with a variable speed button is necessary for a beginner since you can start slowly and then continue at a fast

rate. The speed of a saw that does not have this button cannot be slowed down.

How can you cut out centers?

First, drill a hole at the wood's head and then remove the blade from its clamp on the scroll saw. Then, pass the blade through the hole and then fix it back to the saw clamp. And when you are done cutting, power off your saw first before you unclamp the blade and then pass it free from the wood.

What is causing my blades to break more rapidly than ever before?

If you feed the wood too quickly to the running blade, it could end up breaking. You could also be putting a lot of pressure on the blade by trying to rush things up. Bigger blades are meant to cut through hardwoods, while smaller ones can only cut through softwoods. Interchanging one for the other will only cause your blade to break even faster.

Conclusion

Now that you have learned everything to know about the scroll saw device, ensure that you carry out the projects listed in this outline. When you are done with each, observe the cuttings and edges of the project. If you see that there are many irregularities, repeat the project repeatedly until you get your desired result.

The more you practice, the better you get.

Happy scrolling, scroll artists!

www.ingramcontent.com/pod-product-compliance
Lightning Source LLC
Chambersburg PA
CBHW050944050726
47592CB00007B/2422